The Physiology Of Taste;

Or,

Transcendental Gastronomy

Illustrated By Anecdotes Of Distinguished Artists And Statesmen Of Both Continents

By

Brillat Savarin

Translated From The Last Paris Edition By Fayette Robinson

erchant Books

1825

CONTENTS

BIOGRAPHICAL SKETCH

The excellent man to whom we are indebted for this book has described himself, with so much charm, nature and truth; the principal events of his life have been recorded in such an agreeable and faithful manner that very few words will suffice to finish the story.

Brillat Savarin (Anthelme) Counsel of the Court of Cassation, member of the Legion of Honor, member of the Society for the Encouragement of National Industry, of the Antiquarian Society of France, of the Philoselic Society of Bourg, &c., &c., was born, 1st of April, 1755, at Belley, a little Alpine city, not far from the banks of the Rhine, which at this place separates France from Savoy. Like his forefathers, who had been for several generations devoted to the bar, the profession which pleased him, in consequence of his possession of great eloquence, he practiced with great success.

In, 1789, the unanimous vote of his fellow citizens deputed him to the Constituent assembly, composed of all that was most brilliant in the youth of France at that day. Less attached in practice to the philosophy of Zeno than that of Epicurus, his name does not figure very conspicuously, but always appears at epochs, which show that he acted with the good and moderate.

His legislative functions being determined by the expiration of the Constituent Assembly, he was first appointed President of the Superior Civil court of the Department of Ain, and subsequently a Justice of the Court of Cassation, newly instituted; a man of talent, perfectly incorruptible and unhesitating in the discharge of his duty, he would have been precisely calculated for the place to which he had been appointed, had the warmth of political discussion made practicable the advice either of moderation or of prudence. In 1793, he was Mayor of Belley, and passed in anxiety there, the season of the reign of Terror; whence he was forced to fly to Switzerland for an asylum against the revolutionary movement. Nothing can better man, without a personal enemy, should be forced to pass in a foreign land the days he purposed to devote to the improvement of his country.

This is the point when the character of Brillat Savarin assumes its grandest proportions; proscribed, a fugitive, and often without pecuniary resources, frequently unable to provide for his personal safety, he was always able to console his companions in exile and set them an example of honest industry. As time rolled on, and his situation became more painful, he sought to find in the new world a repose which Europe denied him; he came from Europe, and in Boston, New York, Philadelphia, and Hartford passed two years teaching the French language, and for a time playing the first violin in the orchestra of the Park Theatre. Like many other emigres, Brillat Savarin ever sought to make the pleasant and the useful coincide. He always preserved very pleasant recollection of this period of his life, in which he enjoyed, with moderate labor, all that is necessary for happiness, liberty sweetened by honest toil. He might say all is well, and to be able to enjoy the breath of my native land would alone increase my happiness; he fancied that he saw brighter days with the commencement of Vendémiaire year 5, corresponding to September, of 1796. Appointed by the Directory, as Secretary of the General in Chief of the Republican armies in Germany, then Commisary of the government in the department of the Seine and Oise, (this appointment he held at the epoch of the 18th Brumaire, in which France fancied she exchanged liberty for repose,) sustained by the Senate and the Court, Brillat Savarin passed the remaining twenty-five years of his life respected by his inferiors, loved by his equals, and honored by all. A man of mind, a pleasant guest, with a deep fund of humor, he delighted every body. His judicial labors did not at all interfere with the composition of this book, which he esteemed the great one of his life.

To the very facility of its composition, the "Physiology of the Taste," owes its success; one would form a very erroneous opinion of it, were he to estimate it at all as we do Montaigue's writings on the Gueule. Savarin was naturally a thoughtful man, the simplest meal satisfied him, all he required was that it should be prepared artistically; and he maintained that the art of cookery consisted in exciting the taste. He used to say, "to excite a stomach of Papier Mache, and enliven vital powers almost ready to depart, a cook needs more talent than he who has solved the *infinitesimal calculus*."

The world was much surprised by finding in a book by Brillat Savarin, a man it had always looked upon as simply a very pleasant person, such a vast collection of general information; after his laborious profession he had always seemed to expend the rest of his time with the muses and graces, and none could divine where he obtained so much information, as almost to recall the story of some gray-haired sage of Greece. He had however already composed more than one work unrecognised, if we accept the two opuscula "Critical and Historical Essay on Duel, with Relation to our Legislation and Morals," and a work on judicial practice. They were successful, but he was just then attacked by a violent cold, contracted by being present at the annual ceremony,[1] the 21st of January at the Church of St. Dennis. In spite of every care and attention, on the 2d of February, 1826, he died. For many years gifted with robust health and athletic constitution, made the more remarkable by his tall stature, Brillat Savarin had a presentiment of the approach of death; this feeling, however, did not influence the tenor of his life, for his habitual gaity was maintained unimpaired. When the fatal point was reached, he died *tanquam convivia satur*, not without regret, certainly, for he left many kind friends to whom his memory could not but be dear.

---

[1] Not only Brillat Savarin, but Robert De St. Vincent, and Attorney General Marchangy, contracted their death in consequence of the same ceremonial.

APHORISMS OF THE PROFESSOR

TO SERVE AS PROLEGOMENA TO HIS WORK
AND ETERNAL BASIS TO THE SCIENCE

I. The universe would be nothing were it not for life and all that lives must be fed.

II. Animals fill themselves; man eats. The man of mind alone knows how to eat.

III. The destiny of nations depends on the manner in which they are fed.

IV. Tell me what kind of food you eat, and I will tell you what kind of man you are.

V. The Creator, when he obliges man to eat, invites him to do so by appetite, and rewards him by pleasure.

VI. *Gourmandise* is an act of our judgment, in obedience to which, we grant a preference to things which are agreeable, over those which nave not that quality.

VII. The pleasure of the table belongs to all ages, to all conditions, to all countries, and to all æras; it mingles with all other pleasures, and remains at last to console us for their departure.

VIII. The table is the only place where one does not suffer, from *ennui* during the first hour.

IX. The discovery of a new dish confers more happiness on humanity, than the discovery of a new star.

X. Those persons who suffer from indigestion, or who become drunk, are utterly ignorant of the true principles of eating and drinking.

XI. The order of food is from the most substantial to the lightest.

XII. The order of drinking is from the mildest to the most foamy and perfumed.

XIII. To say that we should not change our drinks is a heresy; the tongue becomes saturated, and after the third glass yields but an obtuse sensation.

XIV. A dessert without cheese is like a beautiful woman who has lost an eye.

XV. A cook may be taught, but a man who can roast, is born with the faculty.

XVI. The most indispensable quality of a good cook is promptness. It should also be that of the guests.

XVII. To wait too long for a dilatory guest, shows disrespect to those who are punctual.

XVIII. He who receives friends and pays no attention to the repast prepared for them, is not fit to have friends.

XIX. The mistress of the house should always be certain that the coffee be excellent; the master that his *liquors* be of the first quality.

XX. To invite a person to your house is to take charge of his happiness as long as he be beneath your roof.

DIALOGUE

between
the author and his friend.
(*after the usual salutations.*)

FRIEND. As my wife and myself were at breakfast this morning, we came to the conclusion that you should print, as soon as possible, your *Gastronomical Observations.*

AUTHOR. What the wife wishes God wills. In six words that is the charta of Paris. I, though, am not subject to that law, for I am an unmarried man.

FRIEND. Bachelors, though, are as subject to the law as others are, sometimes much to our injury. Single blessedness here, however, will not save you. My wife says she has a right to order, because you began your book at her country-house.

AUTHOR. You know, dear Doctor, how I defer to the ladies; more than once you have found my submission to their orders. You also were one of those who said I would make an excellent husband. I will not, however, print my book.

FRIEND. Why not?

AUTHOR. Because being devoted, from the nature of my profession, to serious studies, I fear that those who only know the title of my book will think that I devote myself to trifles.

FRIEND. A panic terror! Thirty-six years of constant toil and labor for the public, have made you a reputation. Besides, my wife and I think every body would read you.

AUTHOR. Indeed!

FRIEND. The learned will read your book to ascertain what you have to tell.

AUTHOR. Perhaps.

FRIEND. Women will read your book because they will see—-

AUTHOR. My dear friend, I am old, I am attacked by a fit of wisdom. *Miserere mei.*

FRIEND. Gourmands will read you because you do them justice, and assign them their suitable rank in society.

AUTHOR. Well, that is true. It is strange that they have so long been misunderstood; I look on the dear *Gourmands* with paternal affection. They are so kind and their eyes are so bright.

FRIEND. Besides, did you not tell me such a book was needed in every library.

AUTHOR. I did. It is the truth—and I would die sooner than deny it.

FRIEND: Ah! you are convinced! You will come home with me?

AUTHOR. Not so. If there be flowers in the author's path, there are also thorns. The latter I leave to my heirs.

FRIEND. But then you disinherit your friends, acquaintances and cotemporaries. Dare you do so?

AUTHOR. My heirs! my heirs! I have heard that shades of the departed are always flattered by the praise of the living; this is a state of beatitude I wish to reserve myself for the other world.

FRIEND. But are you sure that the praise you love so, will come to the right address? Are you sure of the exactness of your heirs?

AUTHOR. I have no reason to think they will neglect a duty, in consideration of which I have excused them the neglect of so many others.

FRIEND. Will they—can they have for your book the paternal love, the author's attention without which every work always comes awkwardly before the public?

AUTHOR. My manuscript will be corrected, written out distinctly, and in all respects prepared; they will only have to print it.

FRIEND. And the chapter of events? Alas! such circumstances have caused the loss of many precious books,—among which was that of the famous Lecat, on the state of the body during sleep, the work of his whole life.

AUTHOR. This doubtless was a great loss; but I anticipate no such regrets for my book.

FRIEND. Believe me, your friends will have enough to do-to arrange matters with the church, with the law, and with the medical faculty, so that if they had the will, they would not have the time to devote them-selves to the various cares which precede, accompany, and follow the publication of a book,—however small the volume may be.

AUTHOR. But, my friend, what a title! Think of the ridicule!

FRIEND. The word Gastronomy makes every ear attentive; the subject is a la mode, and those who laugh are as great votaries of the science as any others are. This should satisfy you. Do you remember too, that the greatest men have sometimes written books on very trivial subjects,-Montesquieu, for example. [2]

AUTHOR. (*Quickly.*) On my word, that is true. He wrote the Temple of Gnidus, and it would not be difficult to sustain that there is more real utility in meditating on what is at once a necessity, a pleasure, and an occupation every day of our lives, than in telling what was done and said a thousand years ago by two mad people, one of whom pursued through the woods of Greece the other, who had not the least disposition to escape.

FRIEND. Ah! ha! Now you yield?

AUTHOR. Not I. The ass's ear of the author only was shown; and this recalls to my memory a scene of English comedy, which amused me very much; it is, I think, in the play called the Natural Daughter. You shall see, however, for yourself. [3]

The subject relates to the Quakers, that sect which uses "thee" and "thou" to everybody, which dresses simply, never go to war, never swear or act with passion, and who never get angry. The hero of this piece is a young and handsome Quaker, who appears on the scene in a brown coat, a broad-brimmed hat, and slick hair! All this, though, does not keep him from being in love.

A fool who is his rival, emboldened by his exterior, ridicules and outrages him so that the young man gradually becoming excited, and finally made furious, gives his assailant a severe thrashing.

Having done this he at once resumes his habitual deportment and says, sadly, "Alas! the flesh is too mighty for the spirit."

Thus say I, and after a brief hesitation resume my first opinion.

---

[2] M. de Monjucla, known as the author of an excellent history of mathematics, made a Dictionary of Gourmand Geography; he showed me portions of it during my residence at Versailles. It is said that M. Berryat-Professor of legal practice, has written a romance in several volumes on the subject.

[3] The reader will observe that my friend permits me to be familiar with him, without taking advantage of it. The reason is, that the difference between our ages is that of a father and a son, and that, though now a man of great note and importance in every respect, he would be completely overcome with grief if I changed my bearing towards him.

FRIEND. That is impossible. You have shown your ear; you are a prize, and I will take you to my bookseller. I will tell you who has gotten wind of your secret.

AUTHOR. Do not; for I would speak of yourself, and who knows what I would say?

FRIEND. What could you say? Do not think you can intimidate me.

AUTHOR. I will not say that our native city[4] is proud of having given you birth. At the age of twenty-four you published an elementary book, which from that day has become a classic. A deserved reputation has attracted confidence to you. Your skill revives invalids; your dexterity animates them; your sensibility consoles them. All know this; but I will reveal to all Paris, to all France, the sole fault of which I know you guilty.

FRIEND. (*Seriously.*) What do you mean?

AUTHOR. An habitual fault which no persuasion can correct.

FRIEND. Tell me what you mean! Why torment me?

AUTHOR. You eat too quickly.

(Here, the friend takes up his hat and leaves, fancying that he has made a convert.)

---

[4] Belley, capital of Bugey, where high mountains, hills, vines, limpid streams, cascades, dells, gardens of a hundred square leagues are found, and where, BEFORE the revolution, the people were able to control the other two orders.

BIOGRAPHY

The Doctor I have introduced into the dialogue we have just read, is not a creature of imagination like the Chloris of other days, but a real living Doctor. Those who know me, will remember RICHERAND.

When I thought of him I could not but have reference to those who preceded him, and I saw with pride that from Belley, from the department of Ain, my native soil, for a long time physicians of the greatest distinction had come. I could not resist the temptation to erect a brief monument to them.

During the regency Doctors Genin and Civoct were in full possession of practice, and expended in their country a wealth they had honorably acquired. The first was altogether HIPPOCRATITE; he proceeded *secundum artem*; the second was almost monopolized by women, and had as his device, as Tacitus would have said, *res novas molientem.*

About 1780 Chapelle became distinguished in the dangerous career of a military surgeon. About 1781 Doctor Dubois had great success in sundry maladies, then very much a la mode, and in nervous diseases. The success he obtained was really wonderful.

Unfortunately he inherited a fortune and became idle, and was satisfied to be a good story-teller. He was very amusing, and contrived to survive the dinners of the new and old regime.[5] About the end of the reign of Louis XV., Dr. Coste, a native of Chatillon came to Paris; he had a letter from Voltaire to the Duc de Choiseuil, the good wishes of whom he gained as soon as he had seen him.

Protected by this nobleman, and by the Duchess of Grammont, his sister, young Coste advanced rapidly, and in a short time became one of the first physicians of Paris.

The patronage he had received took him from a profitable career to place him at the head of the medical department of the army which France sent to the United States, who then were contending for their independence.

---

[5] I smiled when I wrote the above, for it recalled to me an Academician, the eulogium of whom Fontenelle undertook. The deceased knew only how to play at all games. Fontenelle made a very decent oration, however, about him.

Having fulfilled his mission, Coste returned to France, and almost unseen lived through the evil days of 1793. He was elected maire of Versailles, and even now the memory of his administration, at once mild, gentle and paternal, has been preserved.

The Directors now recalled him to the charge of the medical department of the army. Bonaparte appointed him one of the three Inspectors General of the service; the Doctor was always the friend, protector, and patron of the young men who selected that service. He was at last appointed Physician of the Invalides, and discharged the duties until he died.

Such service the Bourbons could not neglect, and Louis XVIII. granted to Doctor Coste the cordon of Saint Michel.

Doctor Coste died a few years since, leaving behind kind recollections, and a daughter married to M. Lalot, who distinguished himself in the Chamber of Deputies by his eloquent and profound arguments.

One day when we had dined with M. Favre, the *Curé* of St. Laurent, Doctor Coste told me of a difficulty he had, the day before, with the Count de Le Cessac, then a high officer of the ministry of war, about a certain economy which the latter proposed as a means of paying his court Napoleon.

The economy consisted in retrenching the allowances of hospital, so as to restrict men who had wounds from the comforts they were entitled to.

Doctor Coste said such measures were abominable, and he became angry.

I do not know what the result was, but only that the sick soldiers had their usual allowances, and that no change was made.

He was appointed Professor of the Faculty of Medicine. His style was simple and his addresses were plain and fruitful. Honors were crowded on him. He was appointed Physician to the Empress Marie Louise. He did not, however, fill that place long, the Emperor was swept away, and the Doctor himself succumbed to a disease of the leg, to which he had long been subject.

Bordier was of a calm disposition, kind and reliable.

About the 18th century appeared Bichat, all of the writings of whom bear the impress of genius. He expended his life in toil to advance science, and joined the patience of restricted minds to enthusiasm. He died at the age of thirty, and public honors were decreed to his memory.

At a later day came Doctor Montegre, who carried philosophy into clinics. He was the editor of the Gazette de Sante, and at the age of forty died in the Antilles whither he had gone to complete his book on the *Vomite Negro.*

At the present moment Richerand stands on the highest degree of operative medicine, and his Elements of Physiology have been translated into every language. Appointed at an early date a Professor of the Faculty of Paris, he made all rely fully on him. He is the keenest, gentlest, and quickest operator in the world.

Recamier, a professor of the same faculty, sits by his side.

The present being thus assured, the future expands itself before us! Under the wings of these mighty Professors arise young men of the same land, who seek to follow their honorable examples.

Janin and Manjot already crush the pavement of Paris. Manjot devotes himself to the diseases of children; he has happy inspirations, and soon will tell the public what he has discovered.

I trust my readers will pardon this digression of an old man, who, during an absence of thirty years, has neither forgotten his country nor his countrymen. I could not however omit all those physicians, the memory of whom is yet preserved in their birth- place, and who, though not conspicuous, had not on that account the less merit or worth.[6]

---

[6] The translator thinks several have made world-renowned names.

PREFACE

In offering to the public the work I now produce, I have undertaken no great labor. I have only put in order materials I had collected long ago. The occupation was an amusing one, which I reserved for my old age.

When I thought of the pleasures of the table, under every point of view, I saw that something better than a common cookery book could be made out of it, and that much might be said about essential and continuous things, which have a direct influence on health, happiness, and even on business.

When I had once gotten hold of the idea, all the rest came naturally. I looked around, took notes, and amidst the most sumptuous festivals looked at the guests. Thus I escaped many of the dangers of conviviality.

To do what I have undertaken, one need not be a physician, chemist, physiologist, or even a savant. All I learned, I learned without the least idea that I would ever be an author. I was impressed by a laudable curiosity, by the fear of remaining behind my century, and by an anxiety to be able to sit at table on equal terms with the savants I used to meet.

I am essentially an amateur medecin, and this to me is almost a mania. Among the happiest days of my life, when with the Professors, I went to hear the thesis of Doctor Cloquet; I was delighted when I heard the murmur of the students' voices, each of whom asked who was the foreign professor who honored the College with his presence.

One other day is, I think, almost as dear to me. I refer to the meeting of the society for the encouragement of national industry, when I presented the *irrorator*, an instrument of my own invention, which is neither more nor less than a forcing pump filled with perfumes.

I had an apparatus fully charged in my pocket. I turned the cock, and thence pressed out a perfume which filled the whole room.

Then I saw, with inexpressible pleasure, the wisest heads of the capital bend beneath my irrigation, and I was glad to see that those who received most, were the happiest.

Thinking sometimes of the grave lucubrations to which I was attracted by my subject, I really as afraid that I would be troublesome. I have often read very stupid books.

I did all that I could to escape this reproach. I have merely hovered over subjects which presented themselves to me; I have filled my book with anecdotes, some of which to a degree are personal. I have omitted to mention many strange and singular things, which critical judgment induced me to reject, and I recalled popular attention to certain things which savants seemed to have reserved to themselves. If, in spite of all these efforts, I have not presented to my readers a science rarely understood, I shall sleep just as calmly, being certain that the MAJORITY will acquit me of all evil intention.

It may perhaps be said that sometimes I wrote too rapidly, and that sometimes I became garrulous. Is it my fault that I am old? Is it my fault that, like Ulysses, I have seen the manners and customs of many cities? Am I therefore blamable for writing a little bit of autobiography? Let the reader, however, remember that I do not inflict my political memoirs on him, which he would have to read, as he has many others, since during the last thirty years I have been exactly in the position to see great men and great things.

Let no one assign me a place among compilers; had I been reduced thus low, I would have laid down my pen, and would not have lived less happily.

I said, like Juvenal:

"Semper ego auditor tantum! nunquamne reponam!"

and those who know me will easily see that used to the tumult of society and to the silence of the study I had to take advantage of both one and the other of these positions.

I did too many things which pleased me particularly; I was able to mention many friends who did not expect me to do so, and recalled some pleasant memories; I seized on others which would have escaped, and, as we say familiarly, took my coffee.

It may be a single reader may in some category exclaim,——"I wished to know if——." "What was he thinking of," etc., etc. I am sure, though, the others will make him be silent and receive with kindness the effusions of a praiseworthy sentiment.

I have something to say about my style, which, as Buffon says, is all the man.

Let none think I come to ask for a favor which is never granted to those who need it. I wish merely to make an explanation.

I should write well, for Voltaire, Jean Jacques, Fenelon, Buffon, and Cochin and Aguesseau were my favorite authors. I knew them by heart.

It may be though, that the gods ordered otherwise; if so, this is the cause of the will of the gods.

I know five languages which now are spoken, which gives me an immense refectory of words.

When I need a word and do not find it in French, I select it from other tongues, and the reader has either to understand or translate me. Such is my fate.

I could have acted otherwise, but was prevented by a kind of system to which I was invincibly attached.

I am satisfied that the French language which I use is comparatively poor. What could I do? Either borrow or steal.

I did neither, for such borrowings, cannot be restored, though to steal words is not punishable by the penal code.

Any one may form an idea of my audacity when I say I applied the Spanish word *volante* to any one I had sent on an errand, and that I had determined to GALLICISE the English word TO SIP, which means to drink in small quantities. I however dug out the French word *siroter*, which expresses nearly the same thing.

I am aware the purists will appeal to Bosseux, to Fenelon, Raceri, Boilleau, Pascal, and others of the reign of Louis XIV. I fancy I hear their clamor.

To all this I reply distinctly, that I do not depreciate the merit of those authors; but what follows? Nothing, except that if they played well on an inferior instrument, how much better would they have done on a superior one. Therefore, we may believe that Tartini would have played on the violin far better than he did, if his bow had been long as that of Baillot.

I do not belong to the *neologues* or even to the romanticists; the last are discoverers of hidden treasures, the former are like sailors who go about to search for provisions they need.

The people of the North, and especially the English, have in this respect an immense advantage over us. Genius is never restricted by the want of expression, which is either made or created. Thus it is that of all subjects which demand depth and energy, our translations make but pale and dull infusions.

Once I heard at the institute a pleasant discourse on the danger of neologism, and on the necessity of maintaining our language as it was when the authors of the great century wrote.

"Like a chemist, I sifted the argument and ascertained that it meant:

"We have done so well, that we neither need nor can do better."

Now; I have lived long enough to know that each generation has done as much, and that each one laughs at his grandfather.

Besides, words must change, when manners and ideas undergo perpetual modifications. If we do things as the ancients did, we do not do them in the same manner. There are whole pages in many French books, which cannot be translated into Latin or Greek.

All languages had their birth, their apogee and decline. None of those which have been famous from the days of Sesostris to that of Philip Augustus, exist except as monuments. The French will have the same fate, and in the year 2825 if read, will be read with a dictionary.

I once had a terrible argument on this matter with the famous M. Andrieux, at the *Academie Francaise*.

I made my assault in good array, I attacked him vigorously, and would have beaten him had he not made a prompt retreat, to which I opposed no obstacle, fortunately for him, as he was making one letter of the new lexicon.

I end by one important observation, for that reason I have kept it till the last.

When I write of ME in the singular, I gossip with my reader, he may examine, discuss, doubt or laugh; but when I say WE I am a professor, and all must bow to me.

> "I am, Sir Oracle,
> And when I ope my lips, let no dog bark."
> *Merchant of Venice*

PHYSIOLOGY OF TASTE

MEDITATION FIRST

THE SENSES

The senses are the organs by which man places himself in connexion with exterior objects.

NUMBER OF THE SENSES

1. They are at least six–

Sight, which embraces space, and tells us by means of light, of the existence and of the colors of the bodies around us.

Hearing, which, by the motion of the air, informs us of the motion of sounding or vibrating bodies.

Scent, by means of which we are made aware of the odors bodies possess.

Taste, which enables us to distinguish all that has a flavor from that which is insipid.

Touch informs us of the consistency and resistance of bodies.

The last is genesiac or physical love, which attracts the sexes to each other, and the object of which is the reproduction of the species.

It is astonishing that, almost to the days of Buffon, so important a sense was misunderstood, and was confounded with the touch.

Yet the sensation of which it is the seat, has nothing in common with touch; it resides in an apparatus as complete as the mouth or the eyes, and what is singular is that each sex has all that is needed to experience the sensation; it is necessary that the two should be united to reach nature's object. If the TASTE, the object of which is the preservation of the individual, be incontestibly a sense, the same title must indubitably be preserved on the organs destined to the preservation of the species.

Let us then assign to the genesiac the sensual place which cannot be refused to it, and let us leave to posterity the assignment of its peculiar rank.

ACTION OF THE SENSES

If we were permitted, even in imagination, to refer to the first moments of the existence of the human race, we would believe that the first sensations were direct; that is to say that all saw confusedly and indirectly, smelled without care, ate without tasting, etc.

The centre of all these sensations, however, being the soul, the sensual attribute of humanity and active cause of perfectibility, they are reflected, compared, and judged by it; the other senses then come to the assistance of each other, for the utility and well-being of the sensitive; one or individual.

Thus touch rectifies the errors of sight; sound, by means of articulate speech, becomes the interpreter of every sentiment; taste is aided by sight and smell; hearing compares sounds, appreciates distance; and the genesiac sense takes possession of the organs of all the senses.

The torrent of centuries rolling over the human race, has continually brought new perfections, the cause of which, ever active though unseen, is found in the demands made by our senses, which always in their turns demand to be occupied.

Sight thus gave birth to painting, to sculpture, and to spectacles of every kind.

Sound, to melody, harmony, to the dance, and to music in all its branches, and means of execution.

Smell, to the discovery, manufacture and use of perfumes.

Taste, to the production, choice and preparation of all that is used for food.

Touch, to all art, trades and occupations.

The genesiac sense, to all which prepares or embellishes the reunion of senses, and, subsequently to the days of Francois I., to romantic love, to coquetry, which originated in France and obtained its name there, and from which the elite of the world, collected in the capital of the universe, take their lessons every day.

This proposition, strange as it seems, is very susceptible of demonstration; we cannot express with clearness in any ancient language, ideas about these three great motives of actual society.

I had written a dialogue on this subject, but suppressed it for the purpose of permitting the reader, each in his own way, to think of the matter for himself. There is enough to occupy the mind and display intelligence and erudition during a whole evening.

We said above, that the genesiac sense took possession of the organs of all the others; the influence it has exerted over all sciences is not less. When we look closer, we will find that all that is most delicate and ingenious is due to the desire, to hope, or to gratitude, in connexion with the union of the sexes.

Such is, indeed, the genealogy of the senses, even the most abstract ones, all being the immediate result of continuous efforts made to gratify our senses.

PERFECTNESS OF THE SENSES

These senses, our favorites, are far from being perfect, and I will not pause to prove it. I will only observe, that that ethereal sense–sight, and touch, which is at the other extremity of the scale, have from time acquired a very remarkable additional power.

By means of spectacles the eye, so to say, escapes from the decay of age, which troubles almost all the other organs.

The telescope has discovered stars hitherto unknown and inaccessible to all our means of mensuration; it has penetrated distances so great, that luminous and necessarily immense bodies present themselves to us only like nebulous and almost imperceptible spots.

The microscope has made us acquainted with the interior configuration of bodies; or has shown the existence of a vegetation and of plants, the existence of which we were ignorant of.

Animals a hundred thousand times smaller than any visible with the naked eye have been discovered; these animalculae, however, move, feed and multiply, establishing the existence of organs of inconceivable tenuity.

Mechanics have multiplied our power; man has executed all that he could conceive of, and has moved weights nature made inaccessible to his weakness.

By means of arms and of the lever, man has conquered all nature; he has subjected it to his pleasure, wants and caprices. He has overturned its surfaces, and a feeble biped has become king of creation.

Sight and touch, being thus increased in capacity, might belong to some species far superior to man; or rather the human species would be far different had all the senses been thus improved.

We must in the meantime remark, that if touch has acquired a great development as a muscular power, civilization has done almost nothing for it as an organ of sensation. We must, however, despair of nothing, but remember that the human race is yet young, and that only after a long series of years can the senses aggrandise their domain.

For instance. Harmony was only discovered about four centuries ago, and that celestial science is to sound what painting is to colors.

Certainly, the ancients used to sing and accompany themselves in unison. Their knowledge, however, ended there. They knew neither how to decompose sounds, nor to appreciate their relations.[7]

Tone was only reduced to system, and accords measured in the fifteenth century. Only then it was used to sustain the voice and to reinforce the expression of sentiments.

This discovery, made at so late a day, yet so natural, doubled the hearing, and has shown the existence of two somewhat independent faculties, one of which receives sound and the other appreciates resonance.

The German Doctors say that persons sensible of harmony have one sense more than others.

Of those persons to whom music is but a confused mass of sounds, we may remark that almost all sing false. We are forced to think that they have the auditory apparatus so made, as to receive but brief and short undulation, or that the two ears not being on the same diapason, the difference in length and sensibility of these constituent parts, causes them to transmit to the brain only an obscure and undetermined sensation, like two instruments played in neither the same key nor the same measure, and which can produce no continuous melody.

The centuries last passed have also given the taste important extension; the discovery of sugar, and its different preparations, of alcoholic liquors, of wine, ices, vanilla, tea and coffee, have given us flavors hitherto unknown.

Who knows if touch will not have its day, and if some fortuitous circumstance will not open to us thence some new enjoyments? This is especially probable as

---

[7] We are aware that the contrary has been maintained; the idea though cannot be supported. Had the ancients been acquainted with harmony, their writings would have preserved some precise notion on the matter, instead of a few obscure phrases, which may be tortured to mean anything. Besides, we cannot follow the birth and progress of harmony in the monuments left to us; this obligation we owe to the Arabs, who made us a present of the organ, which produces at one time many continuous sounds, and thus created harmony.

tactile sensitiveness exists everywhere in the body, and consequently can everywhere be excited.

THE POWERS OF TASTE

We have seen that physical love has taken possession of all the sciences. In this respect it acts with its habitual tyranny.

The taste is a more prudent measure but not less active faculty. Taste, we say, has accomplished the same thing, with a slowness which ensures its success.

Elsewhere we will consider the march. We may, however, observe, that he who has enjoyed a sumptuous banquet in a hall decked with flowers, mirrors, paintings, and statues, embalmed in perfume, enriched with pretty women, filled with delicious harmony, will not require any great effort of thought to satisfy himself that all sciences have been put in requisition to exalt and to enhance the pleasures of taste.

OBJECT OF THE ACTION OF THE SENSES

Let us now glance at the system of our senses, considered together, and we will see that the Author of creation had two objects, one of which is the consequence of the other,—the preservation of the individual and the duration of the species.

Such is the destiny of man, considered as a sensitive being; all his actions have reference to this double purpose.

The eye perceives external objects, reveals the wonders by which a man is surrounded, and tells him he is a portion of the great whole.

Hearing perceives sounds, not only as an agreeable sensation, but as warnings of the movement of bodies likely to endanger us.

The sense of touch watches to warn us by pain of any immediate lesion.

That faithful servant the hand has prepared his defence, assured his steps, but has from instinct seized objects it thought needed to repair losses caused by the use of life.

The sense of smell explores; deleterious substances almost always have an unpleasant smell.

The taste decides; the teeth are put in action, the tongue unites with the palate in tasting, and the stomach soon commences the process of assimilation.

In this state a strange languor is perceived, objects seem discolored, the body bends, the eyes close, all disappears, and the senses are in absolute repose.

When he awakes man sees that nothing around him has changed, a secret fire ferments in his bosom, a new organ is developed. He feels that he wishes to divide his existence.

This active unquiet and imperious sentiment is common to both sexes. It attracts them together and unites them, and when the germ of a new being is fecundated, the individuals can sleep in peace.

They have fulfilled the holiest of their duties by assuring the duration of the species.[8]

Such are the general and philosophical principles I wished to place before my readers, to lead them naturally to the examination of the organ of taste.

---

[8] Buffon describes, with all the charms of the most brilliant eloquence, the first moments of Eve's existence. Called on to describe almost the same subject, we have drawn but one feature. The reader will complete the picture.

MEDITATION II

TASTE

DEFINITION OF TASTE

Taste is the sense which communicates to us a knowledge of vapid bodies by means of the sensations which they excite.

Taste, which has as its excitement appetite, hunger and thirst, is the basis of many operations the result of which is that the individual believes, develops, preserves and repairs the losses occasioned by vital evaporation.

Organized bodies are not sustained in the same manner. The Author of creation, equally varied in causes and effects, has assigned them different modes of preservation.

Vegetables, which are the lowest in the scale of living things, are fed by roots, which, implanted in the native soil, select by the action of a peculiar mechanism, different subjects, which serve to increase and to nourish them.

As we ascend the scale we find bodies gifted with animal life and deprived of locomotion. They are produced in a medium which favors their existence, and have special and peculiar organs which extract all that is necessary to sustain the portion and duration of life allotted them. They do not seek food, which, on the contrary, comes to seek them.

Another mode has been appointed for animals endowed with locomotion, of which man is doubtless the most perfect. A peculiar instinct warns him of the necessity of food; he seeks and seizes the things which he knows are necessary to satisfy his wants; he eats, renovates himself, and thus during his life passes through the whole career assigned to him.

Taste may be considered in three relations.

In physical man it is the apparatus by means of which he appreciates flavors.

In moral man it is the sensation which the organ impressed by any savorous centre impresses on the common centre. Considered as a material cause, taste is the property which a body has to impress the organ and to create a sensation.

Taste seems to have two chief uses:

1. It invites us by pleasure to repair the losses which result from the use of life.

2. It assists us to select from among the substances offered by nature, those which are alimentary.

In this choice taste is powerfully aided by the sense of smell, as we will see hereafter; as a general principle, it may be laid down that nutritious substances are repulsive neither to the taste nor to the smell.

It is difficult to say in exactly what the faculty of taste consists. It is more complicated than it appears.

The tongue certainly plays a prominent part in the mechanism of degustation—for, being endued with great muscular power, it enfolds, turns, presses and swallows food.

Also, by means of the more or less numerous pores which cover it, it becomes impregnated with the sapid and soluble portions of the bodies which it is placed in contact with. Yet all this does not suffice, for many adjacent parts unite in completing the sensation —viz: jaws, palate, and especially the nasal tube, to which physiologists have perhaps not paid attention enough.

The jaws furnish saliva, as necessary to mastication as to the formation of the digestible mass. They, like the palate, are gifted with a portion of the appreciative faculties; I do not know that, in certain cases, the nose does not participate, and if but for the odor which is felt in the back of the mouth, the sensation of taste would not be obtuse and imperfect.

Persons who have no tongue or who have lost it, yet preserve the sensation of taste. All the books mention the first case; the second was explained to me by an unfortunate man, whose tongue had been cut out by the Algerines for having, with several of his companions, formed a plot to escape from captivity.

I met this man at Amsterdam, where he was a kind of broker. He was a person of education, and by writing was perfectly able to make himself understood.

Observing that his whole tongue, to the very attachment, had been cut away, I asked him if he yet preserved any sense of taste when he ate, and if the sense of taste had survived the cruel operation he had undergone.

He told me his greatest annoyance was in swallowing, (which indeed was difficult;) that he had a full appreciation of tastes and flavors, but that acid and bitter substances produced intense pain.

He told me the abscission of the tongue was very common in the African kingdoms, and was made use of most frequently to punish those thought to be the leaders of any plot, and that they had peculiar instruments to affect it with. I wished him to describe them, but he showed such painful reluctance in this matter, that I did not insist.

I reflected on what he said, and ascending to the centuries of ignorance, when the tongues of blasphemers were cut and pierced, I came to the conclusion that these punishments were of Moorish origin, and were imported by the crusaders.

We have seen above, that the sensation of taste resided chiefly in the pores and feelers of the tongue. Anatomy tells us that all tongues are not exactly alike, there being three times as many feelers in some tongues as in others. This circumstance will explain why one of two guests, sitting at the same table, is delighted, while the other seems to eat from constraint; the latter has a tongue but slightly provided. These are recognized in the empire of the taste—both deaf and dumb.

SENSATION OF TASTE

Five or six opinions have been advanced as to the *modus operandi* of the sensation of taste. I have mine, viz:

The sensation of taste is a chemical operation, produced by humidity. That is to say, the savorous particles must be dissolved in some fluid, so as to be subsequently absorbed by the nervous tubes, feelers, or tendrils, which cover the interior of the gastatory apparatus.

This system, whether true or not, is sustained by physical and almost palpable proofs.

Pure water creates no sensation, because it contains no sapid particle. Dissolve, however, a grain of salt, or infuse a few drops of vinegar, and there will be sensation.

Other drinks, on the contrary, create sensation because they are neither more nor less than liquids filled with appreciable particles.

It would be in vain for the mouth to fill itself with the divided particles of an insoluble body. The tongue would feel by touch the sensation of their presence, but not that of taste.

In relation to solid and savorous bodies, it is necessary in the first place for the teeth to divide them, that the saliva and other tasting fluids to imbibe them, and that the tongue press them against the palate, so as to express a juice, which, when sufficiently saturated by the degastory tendrils, deliver to the substance the passport it requires for admission into the stomach.

This system, which will yet receive other developments, replies without effort to the principal questions which may present themselves.

If we demand what is understood by sapid bodies, we reply that it is every thing that has flavor, which is soluble, and fit to be absorbed by the organ of taste.

If asked how a sapid body acts, we reply that it acts when it is reduced to such a state of dissolution that it enters the cavities made to receive it.

In a word, nothing is sapid but what is already or nearly dissolved.

FLAVORS

The number of flavors is infinite, for every soluble body has a peculiar flavor, like none other.

Flavors are also modified by their simple, double, or multiple aggregation. It is impossible to make any description, either of the most pleasant or of the most unpleasant, of the raspberry or of colocynth. All who have tried to do so have failed.

This result should not amaze us, for being gifted with an infinite variety of simple flavors, which mixture modifies to such a number and to such a quantity, a new language would he needed to express their effects, and mountains of *folios* to describe them. Numerical character alone could label them.

Now, as yet, no flavor has ever been appreciated with rigorous exactness, we have been forced to be satisfied with a limited number of expressions such as SWEET, SUGARY, ACID, BITTER, and similar ones, which, when ultimately analyzed, are expressed by the two following AGREEABLE and DISAGREEABLE, which suffice to make us understood, and indicate the flavor of the sapid substances referred to.

Those who come after us will know more, for doubtless chemistry will reveal the causes or primitive elements of flavors.

INFLUENCE OF SMELLING ON THE TASTE

The order I marked out for myself has insensibly led me to the moment to render to smell the rights which belong to it, and to recognise the important services it renders to taste and the application of flavors. Among the authors I have met with, I recognise none as having done full justice to it.

For my own part, I am not only persuaded that without the interposition of the organs of smell, there would be no complete degustation, and that the taste and the sense of smell form but one sense, of which the mouth is the laboratory and the nose the chimney; or to speak more exactly, that one tastes tactile substances, and the other exhalations.

This may be vigorously defended; yet as I do not wish to establish a school, I venture on it only to give my readers a subject of thought, and to show that I have carefully looked over the subject of which I write. Now I continue my demonstration of the importance of the sense of smell, if not as a constituent portion of taste, at least as a necessary adjunct.

All sapid bodies are necessarily odorous, and therefore belong as well to the empire of the one as of the other sense.

We eat nothing without seeing this, more or less plainly. The nose plays the part of sentinel, and always cries "WHO GOES THERE?"

Close the nose, and the taste is paralyzed; a thing proved by three experiments any one can make:

1. When the nasal membrane is irritated by a violent *coryza* (cold in the head) the taste is entirely obliterated. There is no taste in anything we swallow; yet the tongue is in its normal state.

2. If we close the nose when we eat, we are amazed to see how obscure and imperfect the sense of touch is. The most disgusting medicines thus are swallowed almost without taste.

3. The same effect is observed if, as soon as we have swallowed, instead of restoring the tongue to its usual place, it be kept detached from the palate. Thus the circulation of the air is intercepted, the organs of smell are not touched, and there is no taste.

These effects have the same cause, from the fact that the sense of smell does not co-operate with the taste. The sapid body is appreciated only on account of the juice, and not for the odorous gas which emanates from it.

ANALYSIS OF THE SENSATION OF TASTE

Principles being thus determined, I look on it as certain that taste has given place to sensations of three different orders, viz: DIRECT, COMPLETE and REFLECTED.

Direct sensation is the first perception emanating from the intermediate organs of the mouth, during the time that the sapid body rests on the tongue.

Complete sensation is that composed of the first impression which is created when the food abandons this first position, passes into the back of the mouth, and impresses all the organ with both taste and perfume.

Reflected sensation is the judgment which conveys to the soul the impressions transmitted to it by the organ.

Let us put this system in action by observing what takes place when a man either eats or drinks. Let a man, for instance, eat a peach, and he will first be agreeably impressed by the odor which emanates from it. He places it in his mouth, and acid and fresh flavors induce him to continue. Not, though, until he has swallowed it, does the perfume reveal itself, nor does he till then discover the peculiar flavor of every variety. Some time is necessary for any *gourmet* [9] to say, "It is good, passable, or bad. It is Chambertin, or something else."

It may then be seen that in obedience to principles and practice well understood, true amateurs sip their wine. Every mouthful thus gives them the sum total of pleasure which they would not have enjoyed had they swallowed it at once.

The same thing takes place, with however much more energy, when the taste is disagreeably affected.

Just look at the patient of some doctor who prescribes immense doses of black medicine, such as were given during the reign of Louis XIV.

The sense of smell, like a faithful counsellor, foretells its character. The eyes expand as they do at the approach of danger; disgust is on the lips and the stomach at once rebells. He is however besought to take courage, gurgles his throat with brandy, closes his nose and swallows.

----

[9] Any gentleman or lady, who may please, is at perfect liberty to translate the word gourmet into any other tongue. I cannot. As much may be said of gourmand.– TRANSLATOR.

As long as the odious compound fills the mouth and stuns the organ it is tolerable, but when it has been swallowed the after drops develop themselves, nauseous odors arise, and every feature of the patient expresses horror and disgust, which the fear of death alone could induce him to bear.

If the draught be on the contrary merely insipid, as for instance a glass of water, there is neither taste nor after taste. Nothing is felt, nothing is experienced, it is swallowed, and all is over.

ORDER OF THE IMPRESSIONS OF TASTE

Taste is not so richly endowed as the hearing; the latter can appreciate and compare many sounds at once; the taste on the contrary is simple in its action; that is to say it cannot be sensible to two flavors at once.

It may though be doubled and multipled by succession, that is to say that in the act of swallowing there may be a second and even a third sensation, each of which gradually grows weaker and weaker and which are designated by the words AFTER-TASTE, perfume or fragrance. Thus when a chord is struck, one ear exercises and discharges many series of consonances, the number of which is not as yet perfectly known.

Those who eat quickly and without attention, do not discern impressions of the second degree. They belong only to a certain number of the elect, and by the means of these second sensations only can be classed the different substances submitted to their examination.

These fugitive shadows for a long time vibrate in the organ of taste. The professors, beyond doubt, always assume an appropriate position, and when they give their opinions they always do so with expanded nostrils, and with their necks protruded far as they can go.

ENJOYMENTS DUE TO THE TASTE

Let us now look philosophically at the pleasure and pain occasioned by taste.

The first thing we become convinced of is that man is organized so as to be far more sensible of pain than of pleasure.

In fact the imbibing of acid or bitter substances subjects us to sensations more or less painful, according to their degree. It is said that the cause of the rapid effects of hydrocyanic acid is that the pain is so great as to be unbearable by the powers of vitality.

The scale of agreeable sensations on the other hand is very limited, and if there, be a sensible difference between the insipid and that which flatters the taste, the interval is not so great between the good and the excellent. The following example proves this:—FIRST TERM a *Bouilli* dry and hard. SECOND TERM a piece of veal. THIRD TERM a pheasant done to a turn.

Of all the senses though with which we have been endowed by nature, the taste is the one, which all things considered, procures us the most enjoyments.

1. Because the pleasure of eating is the only one, when moderately enjoyed, not followed, by fatigue.

2. It belongs to all aeras, ages and ranks.

3. Because it necessarily returns once a day, and may without inconvenience be twice or thrice repeated in the same day.

4. It mingles with all other pleasures, and even consoles us for their absence.

5. Because the impressions it receives are durable and dependant on, our will.

6. Because when we eat we receive a certain indefinable and peculiar impression of happiness originating in instinctive conscience. When we eat too, we repair our losses and prolong our lives.

This will be more carefully explained in the chapter we devote to the pleasures of the table, considered as it has been advanced by civilization.

SUPREMACY OF MAN

We were educated in the pleasant faith that of all things that walk, swim, crawl, or fly, man has the most perfect taste.

This faith is liable to be shaken.

Dr. Gall, relying on I know not what examinations, says there are many animals with the gustatory apparatus more developed and extended than man's.

This does not sound well and looks like heresy. Man, *jure divino*, king of all nature, for the benefit of whom the world was peopled, must necessarily be supplied with an organ which places him in relation to all that is sapid in his subjects.

The tongue of animals does not exceed their intelligence; in fishes the tongue is but a movable bone, in birds it is usually a membranous cartilage, and in quadrupeds it is often covered with scales and asperities, and has no circumflex motion.

The tongue of man on the contrary, from the delicacy of its texture and the different membranes by which it is surrounded and which are near to it announces the sublimity of the operations to which it is destined.

I have, at least, discovered three movements unknown to animals, which I call SPICATION, ROTATION and VERRATION (from the Latin verb verro, I sweep). The first is when the tongue, like a PIKE, comes beyond the lips which repress it. The second is when the tongue rotates around all the space between the interior of the jaws and the palate. The third is when the tongue moves up and down and gathers the particles which remain in the half circular canal formed by the lips and gums.

Animals are limited in their taste; some live only on vegetables, others on flesh; others feed altogether on grain; none know anything of composite flavors.

Man is omnivorous. All that is edible is subjected to his vast appetite, a thing which causes gustatory powers proportionate to the use he has to make of them. The apparatus of taste is a rare perfection of man and we have only to see him use it to be satisfied of it.

As soon as any esculent body is introduced into the mouth it is confiscated hopelessly, gas, juice and all.

The lips prevent its retrogression. The teeth take possession of it and crush it. The salva imbibes it; the tongue turns it over and over, an aspiration forces it to the thorax; the tongue lifts it up to suffer it to pass. The sense of smell perceives it *en route*, and it is precipitated into the stomach to undergo ulterior transformations, without the most minute fragment during the whole of this escaping. Every drop every atom has been appreciated.

In consequence of this perfection, gourmandise is the exclusive apanage of man.

This *gourmandise* is even contagious, and we impart it without difficulty to the animals we have appropriated to our use, and which in a manner associate with us, such as elephants, dogs, cats, and parrots even.

Besides taste requiring to be estimated only by the value of the sensation it communicates to the common centre, the impression received by the animal cannot be compared to that imparted to man. The latter is more precise and clear, and necessarily supposes a superior quality in the organ which transmits it.

In fine, what can we desire in a faculty susceptible of such perfection that the gourmands of Rome were able to distinguish the flavors of fish taken above and below the bridge? Have we not seen in our own time, that *gourmands* can distinguish the flavor of the thigh on which the partridge lies down from the other? Are we not surrounded by *gourmets* who can tell the latitude in which any wine ripened as surely as one of Biot's or Arago's disciples can foretell an eclipse?

The consequence then is that we must render to Caesar the things which are Caesar's and proclaim man the great GOURMAND OF NATURE, and not be surprised if the good Doctor does sometimes as Homer did: "Much zumeilen ichlafert der gute."

METHOD OF THE AUTHOR

As yet we have treated the taste only from the physical point of view, and in some anatomical details which none will regret, we have remained *pari passu* with science. This does not however conclude the task we have imposed on ourselves, for from its usual attributes especially does this reparatory sense derive its importance.

We have then arranged in analytical order the theories and facts which compose the *ensemble* of this history, so that instruction without fatigue will result from it.

Thus in the following chapters, we will often show how sensations by repetition and reflection have perfected the organs and extended the sphere of our powers. How the want of food, once a mere instinct, has become a passion which has assumed a marked ascendency of all that belongs to society

We will also say, how all sciences which have to do with the composition of substances, have agreed to place in a separate category all those appreciable to the taste; and how travellers have followed in the same pathway when they placed before us substances nature apparently never meant us to see.

We will follow chemistry to the very moment when it penetrated our subterraneous laboratories to enlighten our PREPARERS, to establish principles, to create methods and to unveil causes which had remained occult.

In fine we will see by the combined power of time and experience that a new science has all at once appeared, which feeds, nourishes, restores, preserves, persuades, consoles, and not content with strewing handsfull of flowers over the individual, contributes much to the power and prosperity of empires.

If, amid the grave lucubrations, a piquante anecdote, or an agreeable reminiscence of a stormy life drips from my pen, we will let it remain to enable the attention to rest for a moment, so that our readers, the number of whom does not alarm us, may have time to breathe. We would like to chat with them. If they be men we know they are indulgent as they are well informed. If women they must be charming.[10]

---

[10] Here the Professor, full of his subject, suffers his hand to fall and rises to the seventh heaven. He ascends the torrent of ages, and takes from their cradle all sciences, the object of which is the gratification of taste. He follows their progress through the night of time and seeing that in the pleasures they procure us, early centures were not so great as those which followed them: he takes his lyre and sings in the Dorian style the elegy which will be found among the varieties at the end of the volume.

MEDITATION III

GASTRONOMY

ORIGIN OF SCIENCES

THE sciences are not like Minerva who started ready armed from the brain of Jupiter. They are children of time and are formed insensibly by the collection of the methods pointed out by experience, and at a later day by the principles deduced from the combination of these methods.

Thus old men, the prudence of whom caused them to be called to the bed-side of invalids, whose compassion taught to cure wounds, were the first physicians.

The shepherds of Egypt, who observed that certain stars after the lapse of a certain period of time met in the heavens, were the first astronomers.

The person who first uttered in simple language the truth, 2 + 2 = 4 created mathematics, that mighty science which really placed man on the throne of the universe.

In the course of the last sixty years, many new sciences have taken their place in the category of our knowledge, among which is stéréotomy, descriptive geometry, and the chemistry of gas.

All sciences cultivated for a long time must advance, especially as the art of printing makes retrogression impossible. Who knows, for instance, if the chemistry of gases will not ultimately overcome those, as yet, rebellious substances, mingle and combine them in proportions not as yet tempted, and thence obtain substances and effects which would remove many restrictions in our powers.

ORIGIN OF GASTRONOMY

Gastronomy has at last appeared, and all the sister sciences have made a way for it.

Well; what could be refused to that which sustains us, from the cradle to the grave, which increases the gratifications of love and the confidence of friendship which disarms hatred and offers us, in the short passage of our lives, the only pleasure which not being followed by fatigue makes us weary of all others.

Certainly, as long as it was confided to merely hired attendants, as long as the secret was kept in cellars, and where dispensaries were written, the results were but the products of an art.

At last, too late, perhaps, savants drew near.

They examined, analyzed, and classified alimentary substances, and reduced them to simple elements.

They measured the mysteries of assimilation, and following most matter in all its metamorphoses saw how it became vivified.

They watched diet in its temporary and permanent effects, for days, months and lives.

They even estimated its influence and thought to ascertain if the savor he impressed by the organs or if it acts without them. From all this they deduced a lofty theory which embraces all mankind, and all that portion of creation which may be animalized.

While all this was going on in the studies of *savants*, it was said in drawing-rooms that the science which fed man was at least as valuable as that which killed him. Poets sang the pleasures of the table and books, the object of which was good cheer, awakened the greatest and keenest interest in the profound views and maxims they presented.

Such were the circumstances which preceded the invention of gastronomy.

DEFINITION OF GASTRONOMY

Gastronomy is a scientific definition of all that relates to man as a feeding animal.

Its object is to watch over the preservation of man by means of the best possible food.

It does so by directing, according to certain principles, all those who procure, search for, or prepare things which may be converted into food.

To tell the truth this is what moves cultivators, vinedressers, fishermen, huntsmen, and the immense family of cooks, whatever title or qualification they bear, to the preparation of food.

Gastronomy is a chapter of natural history, for the fact that it makes a classification of alimentary substances.

Of physics, for it examines their properties and qualities.

Of chemistry, from the various analysis and decomposition to which it subjects them.

Of cookery, from the fact that it prepares food and makes it agreeable.

Of commerce, from the fact that it purchases at as low a rate as possible what it consumes, and displays to the greatest advantage what it offers for sale.

Lastly it is a chapter of political economy, from the resources it furnishes the taxing power, and the means of exchange it substitutes between nations.

Gastronomy rules all life, for the tears of the infant cry for the bosom of the nurse; the dying man receives with some degree of pleasure the last cooling drink, which, alas! he is unable to digest.

It has to do with all classes of society, for if it presides over the banquets of assembled kings, it calculates the number of minutes of ebullition which an egg requires.

The material of gastronomy is all that may be eaten; its object is direct, the preservation of individuals. Its means of execution are cultivation, which produces; commerce, which exchanges; industry, which prepares; and experience, which teaches us to put them to the best use.

DIFFERENT OBJECTS OF GASTRONOMY

Gastronomy considers taste in its pleasures and in its pains. It has discovered the gradual excitements of which it is susceptible; it regularizes its action, and has fixed limits, which a man who respects himself will never pass.

It also considers the action of food or aliments on the moral of man, on his imagination, his mind, his judgment, his courage, and his perceptions, whether he is awake, sleeps, acts, or reposes.

Gastronomy determines the degree of esculence of every alimentary subject; all are not presentable under the same circumstances.

Some can be eaten until they are entirely developed. Such like as capres, asparagus, sucking pigs, squabs, and other animals eaten only when they are young.

Others, as soon as they have reached all the perfection to which they are destined, like melons, fruit, mutton, beef, and grown animals. Others when they begin to decompose, such as snipe, wood- cock and pheasant. Others not until cooking has destroyed all their injurious properties, such as the potato, manioc, and other substances.

Gastronomy classifies all of these substances according to their qualities, and indicates those which will mingle, and measuring the quantity of nourishment they contain, distinguishes those which should make the basis of our repast, from those which are only accessories, and others which, though not necessary, are an agreeable relief, and become the *obligato* accompaniment of convivial gossip.

It takes no less interest in the beverages intended for us, according to time, place and climate. It teaches their preparation and preservation, and especially presents them in an order so exactly calculated, that the pleasure perpetually increases, until gratification ends and abuse begins.

Gastronomy examines men and things for the purpose of transporting, from one country to another, all that deserves to be known, and which causes a well arranged entertainment, to be an abridgement of the world in which each portion is represented.

UTILITY OF GASTRONOMICAL KNOWLEDGE

Gastronomical knowledge is necessary to all men, for it tends to augment the sum of happiness. This utility becomes the greater in proportion as it is used by the more comfortable classes of society; it is indispensable to those who have large incomes, and entertain a great deal, either because in this respect they discharge an obligation, follow their own inclination, or yield to fashion.

They have this special advantage, that they take personal pleasure in the manner their table is kept; they can, to a certain point, superintend the depositories of their confidence, and even on many occasions direct them.

The Prince de Soubise once intended to give an entertainment, and asked for the bill of fare.

The maitre d'hotel came with a list surrounded by *vignettes*, and the first article that met the Prince's eye was FIFTY HAMS. "Bertrand," said the Prince, "I think you must be extravagant; fifty hams! Do you intend to feast my whole regiment?"

"No, Prince, there will be but one on the table, and the surplus I need for my *epagnole*, my *blonds*, garnitures, etc."

"Bertrand, you are robbing me. This article will not do."

"Monsigneur," said the artist, "you do not appreciate me! Give the order, and I will put those fifty hams in a chrystal flask no longer than my thumb."

What could be said to such a positive operation? The Prince smiled, and the hams were passed.

INFLUENCE OF GASTRONOMY IN BUSINESS

In men not far removed from a state of nature, it is well known that all important affairs are discussed at their feasts. Amid their festivals savages decide on war and peace; we need not go far to know that villages decide on all public affairs at the cabinet.

This observation has not escaped those to whom the weightiest affairs are often confided. They saw that a full stomached individual was very different from a fasting one; that the table established a kind of alliance between the parties, and made guests more apt to receive certain impressions and submit to certain influences. This was the origin of political gastronomy. Entertainments have become governmental measures, and the fate of nations is decided on in a banquet. This is neither a paradox nor a novelty but a simple observation of fact. Open every historian, from the time of Herodotus to our own days, and it will be seen that, not even excepting conspiracies, no great event ever took place, not conceived, prepared and arranged at a festival.

GASTRONOMICAL ACADEMY

Such, at the first glance, appears to be the domain of gastronomy, a realm fertile in results of every kind and which is aggrandized by the discoveries and inventions of those who cultivate it. It is certain that before the lapse of many years, gastronomy will have its academicians, courses, professors, and premiums.

At first some rich and zealous gastronomer will establish periodical assemblies, in which the most learned theorists will unite with artists, to discuss and measure the various branches of alimentation.

Soon (such is the history of all academies) the government will intervene, will regularise, protect, and institute; it will seize the opportunity to reward the people for all orphans made by war, for all the Arianas whose tears have been evoked by the drum.

Happy will be the depository of power who will attach his name to this necessary institution! His name will be repeated from age to age with that of Noah, Bacchus, Triptolemus, and other benefactors of humanity; he will be among ministers what Henri IV. was among kings; his eulogy will be in every mouth, though no regulation make it a necessity.

MEDITATION IV

APPETITE

DEFINITION OF APPETITE

MOTION and life occasion in the animal portion of all that lives a constant loss of substance, and the human body, that most complicated machine, would soon be unfit for use, did not Providence provide it with a mark to inform it of the very moment when its power is no longer in equilibrium with its wants.

This monitor is appetite. By this word we understand the first impression of the want of food.

Appetite declares itself by languor in the stomach, and a slight sensation of fatigue.

The soul at the same time busies itself with things analogous to its wants; memory recalls food that has flattered its taste; imagination fancies that it sees them, and something like a dream takes place. This state is not without pleasure, and we have heard many adepts say, with joy in their heart, "What a pleasure it is to have a good appetite, when we are certain of a good meal."

The whole nutritive apparatus is moved. The stomach becomes sensible, the gastric juices are moved and displace themselves with noise, the mouth becomes moist, and all the digestive powers are under arms, like soldiers awaiting the word of command. After a few moments there will be spasmodic motion, pain and hunger.

Every shade of these gradations may be observed in every drawing- room, when dinner is delayed.

They are such in nature, that the most exquisite politeness cannot disguise the symptoms. From this fact I deduced the apothegm, "THE MOST INDISPENSABLE QUALITY OF A GOOD COOK IS PROMPTNESS."

ANECDOTE

I will sustain this grave maxim by the details of an observate, made at an entertainment where I was,

"Quorum magna pars fui,"

and where the pleasures of observation preserved me from the anguish of misery.

I was invited to dine with a high public functionary. The hour was half past five, and at the appointed time all were present. We knew he liked exactness, and always scolded the dilatory.

I was amazed, when I came, at the consternation which pervaded the party. People whispered together, and looked into the courtyard through the window–all betokened something extraordinary.

I approached the one of the guests I thought best able to satisfy my curiosity, and asked him what the news was.

"Alas!" said they, "Monsieur has been sent for to the Council of State; he has just gone, and none know when he will return."

"Is that all!" said I. "Be of good cheer, we will be detained only a quarter of an hour; something particular has happened. All know to-day is his regular dinner, and we will not have to fast." I was not, however, easy, and wished I was away.

The first hour passed well enough, and those who were intimate sat together. Common places were exhausted, and conjectures were formed as to what could have called the Prince to the Tuilleries

At the commencement of the second hour there were many signs of impatience; people looked anxiously at each other and the first who murmured were three or four guests who, finding no place to sit in, were not in a convenient position to wait.

At the third hour, the discontent became general, and every symptom became exaggerated. "When will he return?" said one. "What can he be thinking of?" said another. "This is death," said a third. This question was then put, but not determined, "Shall we go or not?"

At the fourth hour every symptom became aggravated. People stretched out their arms without the slightest regard whether they interrupted their neighbors or not. Unpleasant sounds were heard from all parts of the room, and everywhere the faces of the guests bore the marks of concentration. No one listened to me when I remarked that beyond doubt our absent amphytrion was more unhappy than any one of us.

Our attention was for a moment arrested by an apparition. One of the guests, better acquainted with the house than the others, had gone into the kitchen, and returned panting. His face looked as if the day of judgment had come, and in an almost inarticulate voice, which announced at once both the fear of making a noise and of not being heard, "Monsigneur went away without giving any orders, and happen what may, dinner will not be served until his return."

The terror caused by what he said could not be exceeded by that to be expected at the last trump.

Among the martyrs, the most unfortunate was D'Aigrefeuille, whom all Paris knew. His whole body seemed to suffer, and the agony of Laocoon was marked on his face. Pale, terrified, he saw nothing but sank in a chair, grasped his hands on his round stomach, and closed his eyes, not to sleep but to die.

He did not though. About ten o'clock a carriage drove into the yard. All were on the qui-vive and a arose spontaneously. Hilarity succeeded suffering, and in five minutes we were at the table.

Appetite however was gone, all seemed amazed to sit down to dinner at such an unusual hour; the jaws had not that isochronous measure which announces a regular business. I know many were sufferers thus.

The course to be taken is not to eat immediately after the obstacle has ceased, but to drink a glass of *eau-sucree*, or take a plate of soup to sustain the stomach, and then in ten or fifteen minutes to begin dinner, to prevent the stomach being oppressed by the weight of the aliments with which it is surcharged.

GREAT APPETITES

When we see in early books a description of the preparations made to receive two or three persons, and the enormous masses served up to a single guest, we cannot refuse to think that those who lived in early ages were gifted with great appetites.

The appetite was thought to increase in direct ratio to the dignity of the personage. He to whom the saddle of a five-year-old ox would be served was expected to drink from a cup he could scarcely lift.

Some individuals have existed who testified to what once passed, and have collected details of almost incredible variety, which included even the foulest objects.

I will not inflict these disgusting details on my readers, and prefer to tell them two particular circumstances which I witnessed, and which do not require any great exertion of faith.

About forty years ago, I made a short visit to the cure at Bregnier, a man of immense stature and who had a fearful appetite.

Though it was scarcely noon I found him at the table. Soup and bouilli had been brought on, to these two indispensables had succeeded a leg of mutton *a la Royale*, a capon and a salad.

As soon as he saw me he ordered a plate which I refused, and rightly too. Without any assistance he got rid of every thing, viz: he picked the bone of mutton and ate up all the salad.

They brought him a large white cheese into which he made an angular breach measured by an arc of ninety degrees. He washed down all with a bottle of wine and glass of water, after which he laid down.

What pleased me was to see that during the whole of this business, the venerable pastor did not seem busy. The large mouthfulls he swallowed did not prevent him either from laughing or talking. He dispatched all that was put before him easily as he would have a pair of birds.

So it was with General Bisson who drank eight bottles of wine at dinner every day, and who never appeared the worse for it. He had a glass larger than usual and emptied it oftener. He did not care for that though, for after having swallowed six ounces of fluids he could jest and give his orders as if he had only swallowed a thimble full.

This anecdote recalls to me my townsman, General P. Sibuet, long the chief aide of Napoleon, and who was killed in 1813 at the passage of the Bober.

He was eighteen years old, and had at that time the appetite by which nature announces that its possessor is a perfect man, and went one night into the kitchen of Genin, an inn keeper of Belley, where the old men of the town used to meet to eat chestnuts and drink the new white wine called in the country *vin bourru*.

The old men were not hungry and paid no attention to him. His digestive powers were not shaken though, and he said "I have just left the table, but I will bet that I eat a whole turkey."

"If you eat it I will pay for it," said Bouvier du Bouchet, a rich farmer who was present, "and if you do not I will eat what is left and you shall pay for it."[11]

They set to work at once, and the young athlete at once cut off a wing, he ate it at two mouthfulls and cleaned his teeth by gnawing the bone and drank a glass of wine as an interlude.

He then went into the thigh which he ate and drank another glass of wine to prepare a passage for the rest. The second went the same way, and he had come to the last limb when the unfortunate farmer said, "alas! I see it is all over, but Mr. Sibouet as I have to pay, let me eat a bit."[12]

Prosper was as good a fellow as he was a soldier, and consented. The farmer had the carcass at *spolia opima*, and paid for the fowl with a good grace.

General Sibuet used always to love to tell of this feat of his youth. He said that his admitting the farmer to eat was a pure courtesy, and that he could easily have won the bet. His appetite at forty permitted none to doubt the assertion.

Brillat-Savarin, says in a note, "I quote this fragment of the patois of Bugey with pleasure. In it is found the English *'th* and the Greek *o*, and in the word praou and others, a dipthong existing in no language, the sound of which no character can describe." (*See 3d Volume of the Memoirs of the Royal Society of Antiquarians of France.*)

---

[11] This sentence is patois, and the translator inserts the original. "Sez vosu mezé, z'u payo, répondit Bouvier du Bouchet, gros fermier qui se trouvait présent; è sez vos caca en rotaz, i-zet vo ket paire et may ket mezerai la restaz."

[12] This also is patois. "Hai! ze vaie *praou* qu'izet fotu; m'ez, monche Chibouet, poez kaet zu daive paiet, lessé m'en a m'en mesiet on mocho."

MEDITATION V

FOOD IN GERMS

SECTION FIRST

DEFINITIONS

WHAT is understood by aliments?

POPULAR ANSWER. All that nourishes us.

SCIENTIFIC ANSWER. By aliments are understood the substances which, when submitted to the stomach, may be assimulated by digestion, and repair the losses which the human body is subjected to in life.

The distinctive quality of an aliment, therefore, is its liability to animal assimulation.

ANALYSIS

The animal and vegetable kingdoms are those which until now have furnished food to the human race.

Since analytical chemistry has become a certain science, much progress has been made into the double nature of the elements of which our body is composed, and of the substances which nature appears to have intended to repair their losses.

These studies had a great analogy, for man is to a great degree composed both of the substances on which animals feed, and was also forced to look in the vegetable kingdom for affinities susceptible of animalization.

In these two walks the most praiseworthy efforts have been made always as minute as possible, and the curious have followed either the human body or the food which invigorates it, first to their secondary principles, and then to their elements, beyond which we have not been permitted to penetrate.

Here I intended to have given a little treatise on alimentary chemistry, and to tell my readers, to how many thousands of hydrogen, carbon, etc., may be reduced the dishes that sustain us. I did not do so, however, because I remembered I would only have to copy many excellent treatises on chemistry in the hands of every body. I feared, too, that I would relapse into very barren details, and limited myself to a very reasonable nomenclature, which will only require the explanation of a small number of very usual terms.

OSMAZÔME

The greatest service chemistry has rendered to alimentary science, is the discovery of osmazôme, or rather the determination of what it was.

Osmazôme is the purely sapid portion of flesh soluble in cold water, and separated from the extractive portion which is only soluble in boiling water.

Osmazôme is the most meritorious ingredient of all good soups. This portion of the animal forms the red portion of flesh, and the solid parts of roasts. It gives game and venison its peculiar flavor.

Osmazôme is most abundant in grown animals which have red or black hair; it is scarcely found at all in the lamb, sucking pig, chicken, and the white meat of the largest fowls. For this reason true connoisseurs always prefer the second joint; instinct with them was the precursor of science.

Thus a knowledge of the existence of osmazôme, caused so many cooks to be dismissed, who insisted on always throwing away the first *bouillon* made from meat. This made the reputation of the *soupe des primes*, and induced the canon Chevrier to invent his locked kettles. The Abbe Chevrier was the person who never would eat until Friday, lobsters that had not been cooked on the previous Sunday, and every intervening day placed on the fire with the addition of fresh butter.

To make use of this subject, though yet unknown, was introduced the maxim, that to make good *bouillon* the kettle should only smile.

Osmazôme, discovered after having been so long the delight of our fathers, may be compared to alcohol, which made whole generations drunk before it was simply exhibited by distillation.

PRINCIPLE OF ALIMENTS

The fibre is what composes the tissue of the meat, and what is apparent after the juices have been extracted. The fibres resist boiling water, and preserve their form, though stripped of a portion of their wrappings. To carve meat properly the fibres should be cut at right angles, or nearly so, with the blade of the knife. Meat thus carved looks better, tastes better, and is more easily chewed.

The bones are composed principally of gelatine and the phosphate of lime.

The quantity of gelatine diminishes, as we grow older. At seventy the bones are but an imperfect marble, the reason why they are so easily broken, and why old men should carefully avoid any fall.

Albumen is found both in the flesh and the blood. It coagulates at a heat above 40 Réaumur, and causes the scum on the *pot-au-feu*.

Gelatine is also found in the bones, the soft and the cartilaginous parts. Its distinctive quality is to coagulate at the ordinary temperature of the atmosphere; to affect this only two and a half per cent are needed.

Gelatine is the basis of all jelleys, of *blanc manges*, and other similar preparations.

Grease is a concrete oil formed in the interstices of the cellary tissue. It sometimes agglomerates in animals whom art or nature has so predisposed, such as pigs, fowls, ortolans and snipe. In some of these animals it loses its insipidity and acquires a slight and agreeable aroma.

Blood is composed of an albuminous serum and of fibrine, some gelatine and a little osmazome. It coagulates in warm water and is most nourishing, (*e. g.*) the blood pudding.

All the principles, we have passed in review, are common to man and to animals which feed.

All the principles we pass in review are common both to man and animals which he eats. It is not then surprising that animal food is eminently restorative and invigorating. The particles of which it is composed having a great similitude with those of which we are formed may easily be animalized when they are subjected to the vital action of our digestive organs.

VEGETABLE KINGDOM

The vegetable kingdom however presents not less varied sources of nutrition.

The *fecula* is especially nutritious, especially as it contains fewer foreign principles.

By *fecula* we mean farina or flower obtained from cereals, from *legumes* and various kinds of roots, among which the potato holds a prominent place.

The *fecula* is the substance of bread, pastry and *pureés* of all kinds. It thus enters to a great degree into the nourishment of almost all people.

Such food diminishes the fibres and even the courage.[13] We must, to sustain this, refer to the Indians (East) who live on rice and serve every one who chooses to command them.

Almost all domestic animals eat the *fecula*, and are made by it extremely strong; for it is a more substantial nourishment than the dry and green vegetables which are their habitual food.

Sugar is not less important, either as a remedy or as an aliment.

This substance once obtained, either from the Indies or from the colonies became indigenous at the commencement of this century. It has been discovered in the grape, the turnip, the chestnut, and especially in the beet. So that speaking strictly Europe need appeal neither to India or America for it. Its discovery was a great service rendered by science to humanity, and furnishes an example which cannot but have the happiest results. (*Vide enfro Sugar.*)

Sugar, either in a solid state or in the different plants in which nature has placed it, is extremely nourishing. Animals are fond of it, and the English give large quantities to their blood-horses, and have observed that it sustained them in the many trials to which they were subjected.

Sugar in the days of Louis XIV. was only found in apothecary shops, and gave birth to many lucrative professions, such as pastry-cooks, confectioners, *liquourists*, &c. Mild oils also come from the vegetable kingdom. They are all esculent, but when mingled with other substances they should be looked on only as a seasoning. Gluten found in the greatest abundance in cheese, contributes greatly to the fermentation of the bread with which it is united. Chemists assign it an animal nature.

They make at Paris for children and for birds, and in some of the departments for men also, *patisseries* in which gluten predominates, the *fecula* having been removed by water.

---

[13] The H. E. I. Co. Sepoys, however, fight well. It may be doubted though if either Ireland or Italy will be free, until the one gives up the potato and the other macaroni. The reason why Irishmen fight better in other countries than their own, is possibly that abroad they are better fed than at home.

Mucilage owes its nourishments to the many substances of which it is the vehicle.

Gum may be considered an aliment, not a strong thing, as it contains nearly the same elements as sugar.

Vegetable gelatine, extracted from many kinds of fruits, especially from apples, gooseberries, quinces, and some others, may also be considered a food. It is more nutritious when united with sugar, but it is far inferior in that respect to what is extracted from bones, horns, calves' feet and fish. This food is in general light, mild and healthy. The kitchen and the pharmaceutist's laboratory therefore dispute about it.

DIFFERENCE BETWEEN FAT AND LEAN

Next to the JUICE, which, as we have said, is composed of asmazôme and the *extractus*, there are found in fish many substances which also exist in land animals, such as fibrine, gelatine, albumen. So that we may really say JUICE distinguishes the flesh diet from what the church calls *maigre*.

The latter too has another peculiarity. Fish contains a large quantity of phosphorus and hydrogen, that is to say of the two most combustible things in nature. Fish therefore is a most heating diet. This might legitimate the praise once bestowed on certain religious orders, the regime of whom was directly opposed to the commonly esteemed most fragile.

INDIVIDUAL INSTANCE.

I will say no more on this physiological fact, but will not omit an instance which may be easily verified.

Some years ago I went to a country house, in the vicinity of Paris, and on the Seine, near St. Denis, near a hamlet composed chiefly of fishing huts. I was amazed at the crowd of huts I saw swarming in the road.

I remarked it with amazement to the boatman who took me across the river.

"Monsieur," said he, "we have eight families here, have fifty- three children, among whom are forty-nine girls and four boys. That one is mine." As he spoke he pointed triumphantly to a little whelp, of about five years of age, who was at the bow of the boat eating raw crawfish.

From this observation I made ten years ago, and others I could easily recall, I have been led to think that the genesiac sense is moved by fish-eating, and that it is rather irritating than plethoric and substantial. I am inclined to maintain this opinion the more, because Doctor Bailly has recently proved, by many instances, that whenever the number of female children exceeds the male, the circumstance is due to some debilitating circumstances. This will account to us for the jests made from the beginning of time, whenever a man's wife bears him a daughter instead of a son.

I might say much about aliments considered as a *tout ensemble*, and about the various modifications they undergo by mixing, etc.; I hope, though, that the preceding will suffice to the majority of readers. I recommend all others to read some book *ex professo*, and will end with the things which are not without interest.

The first is that animalization is affected almost as vegetation is, that is that the reparative current formed by digestion, is inhaled in various manners by the tubes with which the organs are provided, and becomes flesh, nails, hair, precisely as earth, watered by the same fluid, becomes radish, lettuce, potato,–as the gardener pleases.

The second is that in the organization of life, the same elements which chemistry produces are not obtained. The organs destined to produce life and motion only act on what is subjected to them.

Nature, however, loves to wrap herself in veils, and to stop us at every advance, and has concealed the laboratory where new transformations are affected. It is difficult to explain how, having determined that the human body contained lime, sulphur, and phosphorous iron, and the other substances, all this CAN be renewed every ten years by bread and water.

MEDITATION VI

FOOD IN GERMS

SECTION SECOND

SPECIALITIES

WHEN I began to write, my table of contents was already prepared; I have advanced slowly, however, because a portion of my time is consecrated to serious labors.

During this interval of time much of my matter has escaped my memory, or been wrested from me. Elementary books on chemistry or materia medica have been put into the hands of every body, and things I expected to teach for the first time, have become popular. For instance, I had devoted many pages to the chemistry of the *pot-au-feu*, the substance of which is found in many books recently published.

Consequently, I had to revise this part of my book, and have so condensed it that it is reduced to a few elementary principles, to theories which cannot be too widely propagated, and to sundry observations, the fruits of a long experience, which I trust will be new to the majority of my readers.

Section I. POT-AU-FEU, POTAGE, ETC.

Pot-au-feu is a piece of beef, intended to be cooked in boiling water, slightly salted so as to extract all the soluble parts.

Bouillon is the fluid which remains after the operation.

Bouilli is the flesh after it has undergone the operation.

Water dissolves at first a portion of the osmazôme; then the albumen coagulates at 50 degrees Réaumur, and forms the foam we see. The rest of the osmazôme, with the extractive part of juice, and finally a portion of the wrapping of the fibres detached by the continuity of ebullition.

To have good bouillon, the water must be heated slowly, and the ebullition must be scarcely perceptible, so that the various particles necessarily dissolved, may unite ultimately and without trouble.

It is the custom to add to bouillon, vegetable or roots, to enhance the taste, and bread or *patés* to make it more nourishing. Then it is what is called *potage*.

Potage is a healthy food, very nourishing, and suits every body; it pleases the stomach and prepares it for reception and digestion. Persons threatened with obesity should take bouillon alone.

All agree that nowhere is potage made so well as in France, and in my travels I have been able to confirm this assertion. Potage is the basis of French national diet, and the experience of centuries has perfected it.

Section II. BOUILLI

Bouilli is a healthful food, which satisfies hunger readily, is easily digested, but which when eaten alone restores strength to a very small degree, because in ebullition the meat has lost much of its *animalizable juices*.

We include in four categories the persons who eat bouilli.

1. Men of routine, who eat it because their fathers did, and who, following this practice implicitly, expect to be imitated by their children.

2. Impatient men, who, abhorring inactivity at the table, have contracted the habit of attacking at once whatever is placed before them.

3. The inattentive, who eat whatever is put before them, and look upon their meals as a labor they have to undergo. All that will sustain them they put on the same level, and sit at the table as the oyster does in his bed.

4. The voracious, who, gifted with an appetite which they seek to diminish, seek the first victim they can find to appease the gastric juice, which devours them, and wish to make it serve as a basis to the different envois they wish to send to the same destination.

Professors of gastronomy never eat bouilli, from respect to the principles previously announced, that bouilli is flesh without the juices.[14]

---

[14] This idea which began to make its impression on bouilli has disappeared. It is replaced by a roasted filet, a turbot, or a matelote.

Section III. FOWLS

I am very fond of second courses, and devoutly believe that the whole gallinaceous family was made to enrich our larders and to deck our tables.

From the quail to the turkey, whenever we find a fowl of this class, we are sure to find too, light aliment, full of flavor, and just as fit for the convalescent as for the man of the most robust health.

Which one of us, condemned to the fare of the fathers of the desert, would not have smiled at the idea of a well-carved chicken's wing, announcing his rapid rendition to civilized life?

We are not satisfied with the flavor nature has given to gallinaceous fowls, art has taken possession of them, and under the pretext of ameliorating, has made martyrs of them. They have not only been deprived of the means of reproduction, but they have been kept in solitude and darkness, and forced to eat until they were led to an unnatural state of fatness.

It is very true that this unnatural grease is very delicious, and that this damnable skill gives them the fineness and succulence which are the delight of our best tables.

Thus ameliorated, the fowl is to the kitchen what the canvass is to painters. To charlatans it is the cap of Fortunatus, and is served up boiled, roasted, fried, hot, cold, whole or dismembered, with or without sauce, broiled, stuffed, and always with equal success.

Three portions of old France disputed for the honor of furnishing the best fowls, viz: Caux, Mans, and Bresse.

In relation to capons, and about this there is some doubt, the one on the table always seeming the best. Bresse seems, however, to have pre-eminence in pullets, for they are round as an apple. It is a pity they are so rare in Paris!

Section IV. THE TURKEY

The turkey is certainly one of the most glorious presents made by the new world to the old.

Those persons who always wish to know more than others, say that the turkey was known to the ancients, and was served up at the wedding feast of

Charlemagne. They say it is an error to attribute the importation to the Jesuits. To these paradoxes but two things can be opposed:

1st. The name of the bird proves its origin, for at one time America was called the West Indies.

2d. The form of the bird is altogether foreign.

A well informed man cannot be mistaken about it.

Though already perfectly satisfied, I made much deep research in the matter. I will not inflict my studies on my readers, but will only give them the results:

1. The turkey appeared in Europe about the end of the seventeenth century.

2. That it was imported by the Jesuits who sent a large number especially to a farm they had near Bouges.

3. That thence they spread gradually over France, and in many localities a turkey to this day is called a Jesuit.

4. Only in America has the turkey been found in a wild state, (it is unknown in Africa.)

5. That in the farms of North America, where it is very common, it has two origins, either from eggs which have been found and hatched or from young turkeys caught in the woods. The consequence is they are in a state of nature and preserve almost all their original plumage.

Overcome by this evidence I bestow on the good fathers a double portion of gratitude, for they imported the Quinquina yet known as "Jesuit's bark."

The same researches informed us that the turkey gradually became acclimated in France. Well informed observers have told me that about the middle of the last century of twenty young turkeys scarcely ten lived, while now fourteen out of every twenty mature. The spring rains are most unfortunate to them; the large drops of rain striking on their tender heads destroy them.

DINDONOPHILES

The turkey is the largest, and if not the finest, at least the most highly flavored of the gallinaceous family.

It has also the advantage of collecting around it every class of society.

When the virgin dresses, and farmers of our countries wish to regale themselves in the long winter evenings, what do they roast before the fire of the room in which the table is spread? a turkey.

When the mechanic, when the artist, collects a few friends to enjoy a relief which is the more grateful because it is the rarer; what is one of the dishes *always* put on the table? a turkey stuffed with Lyons sausage and with chestnuts of Lyons.

In the highest gastronomical circles, in the most select reunions, where politics yield to dissertations on the taste, for what do people wait? What do they wish for? a *dinde truffé* at the second course. My secret memoirs tell me that its flavor has more than once lighted up most diplomatic faces.

FINANCIAL INFLUENCE OF THE TURKEY

The importation of turkeys became the cause of a great addition to the public fortune, and occasioned a very considerable commerce.

By raising turkeys the farmers were able the more surely to pay their rents. Young girls often acquired a very sufficient dowry, and towns-folk who wished to eat them had to pay round prices for them.

In a purely financial point of view turkeys demand much attention.

I have reason to believe, that between the first of November and the end of February, three hundred *dindon truffées* are consumed *per diem*. The sum total is 30,000 turkeys.

The price of every turkey in that condition is at least twenty francs, and the sum of the whole is not less than 720,000 francs– a very pretty sum of money. One must add a similar sum for the fowls, pheasants, pullets and partridges, suffered in the same way, and which are every day exhibited in the provision shops, as a punishment for beholders who are too poor to buy them.

EXPLOIT OF THE PROFESSOR

While I was living at Hartford, in Connecticut, I was lucky enough to kill a wild turkey. This exploit deserves to be transmitted to posterity, and I tell it with especial complaisance as I am myself the hero.

An American farmer had invited me to hunt on his grounds; he lived in the remotest part of the State,[15] and promised me partridges, grey squirrels and wild turkeys.[16] He also permitted me to bring a friend or two if I pleased.

One fine day in October, 1794, therefore, with a friend, I set out with the hope of reaching the farm of Mr. Bulow, five mortal leagues from Hartford, before night.

Though the road was hardly traced, we arrived there without accident, and were received with that cordial hospitality expressed by acts, for before we had been five minutes on the farm, dogs, horses and men were all suitably taken care of.

About two hours were consumed in the examination of the farm and its dependencies. I would describe all this if I did not prefer to display to the reader the four buxom daughters of Mr. Bulow, to whom our arrival was a great event.

Their ages were from sixteen to twenty-four, and there was so much simplicity in their persons, so much activity and abandon, that every motion seemed full of grace.

After our return from walking we sat around a well-furnished table. A superb piece of corned beef, a stewed goose, and a magnificent leg of mutton, besides an abundance of vegetables and two large jugs of cider, one at each end of the table, made up our bill of fare.

When we had proven to our host, that in appetite at least, we were true huntsmen, we began to make arrangements for our sport. He told us where we would find game, and gave us landmarks to guide us on our return, not forgetting farmhouses where we could obtain refreshments.

During this conversation the ladies had prepared excellent tea, of which we drank several cups, and were then shown into a room with two beds, where exercise and fatigue procured us a sound sleep.

On the next day we set out rather late, and having come to the end of the clearings made by Mr. Bulow, I found myself in a virgin forest for the first time. The sound of the axe had never been heard there.

---

[15] Brillat-Savarin uses the French words "*derrières de l'état*" and translates them in English, in parenthesis "Backwoods."
[16] He also translates in the same manner "*dindes sauvages*" welp cocks.

I walked about with delight, observing the blessings and ravages of time which creates and destroys, and I amused myself by tracing all the periods on the life of an oak since the moment when its two leaves start from the ground, until it leaves but a long black mark which is the dust of its heart.

My companion, Mr. King, reproached me for my moodiness, and we began the hunt. We killed first some of those pretty grey partridges which are so round and so tender. We then knocked down six or seven grey squirrels, highly esteemed in America, and at last were fortunate enough to find a flock of turkeys.

They rose one after the other, flying rapidly and crying loudly. Mr. King fired on the first and ran after it. The others were soon out of shot. The most sluggish, of all arose at last, not ten paces from me. It flew through an opening, I fired and it fell dead.

One must be a sportsman to conceive the extreme pleasure this shot caused me. I siezed on the superb bird and turned it over and over for a quarter of an hour, until I heard my companion's voice calling for assistance. I hurried to him and found that he called me to aid him in looking for a turkey he claimed to have killed, but which had disappeared.

I put my dog on the scent but he led us into an under growth, so thick and thorny that a snake could scarcely penetrate it; I had then to give up the search, and my companion was in a bad humor all day long.

The rest of the day scarcely deserves the honors of printing. On our return we lost ourselves in boundless woods, and we were in not a little danger of having to stay out all night, when the silvery tones of Mr. Bulow's daughters, and the deep bass of their father, who had come to look for us, guided us home.

The four sisters were fully armed with clean dresses, new ribbons, pretty hats, and so carefully shod that it was evident that they had formed a high opinion of us. I tried to make myself agreeable to the one of the ladies who took my arm, a thing she did as naturally as if it had belonged to her *jure conjugali*.

When we reached the farm supper was ready, but before we sat down to the table we drew near to a bright and brilliant fire which had been lighted for us, though the season did not indicate that such a a precaution was necessary. We found it very comfortable, fatigued as we were, and were rested as if by enchantment.

This custom doubtless comes from the Indians who always have a fire in their huts. It may be, this is a tradition of St. Francis de Sales, who said that fire was good eleven months of the year (*non liquet*).

We ate as if we were famished; a large bowl of punch enabled us to finish the evening, and a conversation, which our host made perfectly free, led us far into the night.

We spoke of the war of Independence, in which Mr. Bulow[17] had served as a field officer of M. de La Fayette, who every day becomes greater in the eyes of the Americans, who always designate him as "the Marquis" of agriculture, which at that time enriched the United States, and finally of my native land, which I loved the more because I was forced to leave it.

When wearied of conversation the father would say to his eldest daughter, "Maria, give us a song." She without any embarrassment sung the American national airs. The complaints of Mary Stuart and of Andre, all popular in America. Maria had taken a few lessons, and in that remote country passed for a virtuosa; her singing though, derived its charm from the quality of her voice, which was at once clear, fresh and accentuated.

On the next day, in spite of Mr. Bulow's persuasions, we set out. I had duties to discharge; and while the horses were being prepared, Mr. Bulow took me aside and used these remarkable words.

"You see in me, sir, a happy man, if there be one under heaven; all that you see here is derived from my own property. My daughters knit my stockings, and my flocks furnished my cloths. They also, with my garden, furnish me with an abundance of healthy food. The greatest eulogium of our government is, that in the State of Connecticut there are a thousand farmers as well satisfied as I am, the doors of whom have no locks.

"Taxes are almost nothing, and as long as they be paid any one can sleep calmly. Congress favors national industry as much as it can, and merchants are always ready to take from us whatever we wish to sell. I have ready money for a long time, for I have just sold at twenty-four dollars a barrel, flour I usually receive eight for.

---

[17] The M. Bulow of whom Savarin speaks, is none other than Lieut. Col. Bellows of the Connecticut Line, many of whose relations yet remain in the Valley of the Connecticut.

"All this is derived from the liberty we have acquired, and established on good laws. I am master of my own house; and you will not be astonished when you know that we never fear the sound of the drum, and, except on the 4th of July, the glorious anniversary of our Independence, neither soldiers, uniforms, nor bayonets are seen."

On my way back I seemed absorbed by profound reflection. Perhaps the reader may think I mused on my host's parting words; I had very different thoughts, however, for I was studying how I should cook my turkey. I was in some trouble, for I feared I would not find all I needed at Hartford, and wished to make a trophy of my *spolia opima*.

I make a painful sacrifice in suppressing the details of the profound science I exhibited in the preparation of an entertainment, to which I invited several friends. Suffice it to say that the partridge wings were served *en papillote*, and the grey squirrels stewed in madeira.

The turkey, which was our only roast dish, was charming to the sight, flattering to the sense of smell, and delicious to taste. Therefore, until the last fragment was eaten, there were heard around the table, "Very good;" "Exceedingly good;" "Dear sir; what a nice piece."[18]

Section V. GAME

By game we mean all wild animals which are fit to eat, and live in a state of natural liberty.

We say fit to eat, because many animals which are in a state of nature are not fit to eat. Such as foxes, crows, pies, wild-cats, etc. They are called in French Betes puantes vermin.

Game is divided into three series.

---

[18] The flesh of the wild turkey is more highly colored and more perfumed than the domestic fowl. I am glad to learn that my amiable colleague, M. Bosc, had killed many in Carolina, which he found excellent, and far better than those in Europe. He therefore recommends that they be allowed the largest liberty, that they be driven into the woods and fields, to enhance the flavor and bring it as nearly as possible back to the original species.—*Annales d'Agriculture cah. du 28 Fevr. 1821.*

The first contains all birds, from the grive to the smallest of the feathered tribe.

The second ascends from the rail to the snipe, partridge, and pheasant, including the rabbit and the hare; it is divided into three categories, of the marsh, hairy, and feathered.

The third, which bears the name of venison, is composed of the wild-boar, kid, and all other horny-footed cattle.

Game is one of the great luxuries of our tables; it is a healthy, warm, highly-flavored and high tasted flesh, easily digested, whenever one is hungry.

These qualities, however, are not so inherent as not to a certain degree to depend on the skill of the cook. Put some water, salt and beef into a pot, and you can obtain from them a very good soup. Substitute venison for the beef, and the result will not be fit to eat. Butcher's meat, in this respect, has the advantage. Under the manipulation, however, of a skilful cook, game undergoes various modifications and transformations, and furnishes the greater portions of the dishes of the transcendental kitchen.

Game derives, also, a great portion of its value from the soil on which it is fed. The taste of a Perigord partridge is very different from that of one from Sologne, and the hare killed in the vicinity of Paris is a very different dish from one shot on the hills of Valromey or upper Dauphiny. The latter is probably the most perfumed of all beasts.

Among small birds, beyond all doubt, the best is the "beccafico."

It becomes at least as fat as the red-throat or the ortolan, and nature has besides given it a slight bitterness, and a peculiar and exquisite perfume, which enables it to fill and delight all the gustatory organs. Were the beccafico as large as a pheasant, an acre of land would be paid for it.

It is a pity this bird is so rare, that few others than those who live in the southern departments of France, know what it is.[19] Few people know how to eat small birds. The following method was imparted confidentially to me by the Canon Charcot, a gourmand by profession, and a perfect gastronome, thirty years before the word gastronomy was invented:

Take a very fat bird by the bill and sprinkle it with salt, take out the entrailles, I mean gizzard, liver, etc., and put it whole in your mouth. Chew it

---

[19] I am inclined to think the bird is utterly unknown in America.–TRANSLATOR.

quickly, and the result will be a juice abundant enough to permeate the whole organ. You will then enjoy a pleasure unknown to the vulgar.

"Odi profanum vulgus et arceo."
HORACE.

The quail, of all game properly so-called, is the nicest and the most pleasant. A very fat quail is pleasant both to eat, see, and smell. Whenever it is either roasted, or served en *papillote*, a great folly is committed, because its perfume is very volatile, and when ever in contact with a liquid, its flavor is dissolved and lost.

The snipe is a charming bird, but few people know all its charms. It is in its glory only when it has been cooked under the huntsman's eyes; and the huntsman must have killed it. Then the roast is perfected according to rule, and the mouth is inundated with pleasure.

Above the preceding, and above all others, the pheasant should be placed. Few mortals, however, know exactly how to cook it.

A pheasant eaten only a week after its death is not good as a partridge or a pullet, for its merit consists in its aroma.

Science has considered the expansion of this aroma, experience has utilised science, so that a pheasant ready for the spit is a dish fit for the most exalted gourmands.

In the varieties will be found a recipe for roasting a pheasant, *a la Sainte Alliance*. The time has come when this method, hitherto concentrated in a small circle of friends, should be made known for the benefit of humanity. A pheasant with truffles is not good as one would be apt to think it. The bird is too dry to actuate the tubercle, and the scent of the one and the perfume of the other when united neutralize each other—or rather do not suit.

Section VI. FISH

Savants, in other respects orthodox, have maintained that ocean was the common cradle of all that exists, and that man himself sprang from the sea and owes his actual habits to the influence of the air, and the mode of life he has been obliged to adopt.

Be this as it may, it is at least certain, that the waters contain an immense quantity of beings of all forms and sizes, which possess vitality in very different proportions, and according to mode very different from that of warm blooded animals.

It is not less true that water has ever presented an immense variety of aliments, and that in the present state of science it introduces to our table the most agreeable variety.

Fish, less nutritious than flesh and more succulent than vegetables, is a *mezzo termine*, which suits all temperments and which persons recovering from illness may safely eat.

The Greeks and Romans, though they had not made as much progress as we have in the art of seasoning fish, esteemed it very highly, and were so delicate that they could even tell where it had been taken.

Large fish ponds were maintained, and the cruelty of Vellius Pollis who fed his lampreys on the bodies of slaves he caused to be slain is well known. This cruelty Domitian disapproved of but should have punished.

There has been much discussion as to which is the best fish.

The question will never be decided, for as the Spanish proverb says, *sobre los gustos no hai disputa*. Every one is effected in his own way. These fugitive sensations can be expressed by no known character, and there is no scale to measure if a CAT-FISH (!), a sole, or a turbot are better than a salmon, trout, pike, or even tench of six or seven pounds.

It is well understood that fish is less nourishing than meat, because it contains no osmazome, because it is lighter in weight, and contains less weight in the same volume. Shell-fish, and especially oysters, furnish little nutrition, so that one can eat a great many without injury.

It will be remembered that not long ago any well arranged entertainment began with oysters, and that many guests never paused without swallowing a gross (144). I was anxious to know the weight of this advance guard, and I ascertained that a dozen oysters, fluid included, weighed four ounces *averdupois*. Now look on it as certain that the same persons who did not make a whit the worse dinner, on account of the oysters would have been completely satisfied if they had eaten the same weight of flesh or of chicken.

ANECDOTE

In 1798 I was at Versailles as a commissary of the Directory, and frequently met M. Laperte, greffier of the count of the department. He was very fond of oysters, and used to complain that he had never had enough.

I resolved to procure him this satisfaction, and invited him to dine with me on the next day.

He came. I kept company with him to the tenth dozen, after which I let him go on alone. He managed to eat thirty-two dozen within an hour for the person who opened them was not very skilful.

In the interim, I was idle, and as that is always a painful state at the table, I stopped him at the moment when he was in full swing. "Mon cher," said I, "you will not to-day eat as many oysters as you meant–let us dine." We did so, and he acted as if he had fasted for a week.

Muria-Garum

The ancients extracted from fish two highly flavored seasonings, *muria* and *garum.*

The first was the juice of the thuny, or to speak more precisely, the liquid substance which salt causes to flow from the fish.

Garum was dearer, and we know much less of it. It is thought that it was extracted by pressure from the *entrailles* of the *scombra* or mackerel; but this supposition does not account for its high price. There is reason to believe it was a foreign sauce, and was nothing else but the Indian soy, which we know to be only fish fermented with mushrooms.

Certainly, people from their locality are forced to live almost entirely upon fish. They also feed their working animals with it, and the latter from custom gradually grow to like this strange food. They also manure the soil with it, yet always receive the same quantity from the sea which surrounds them.

It has been observed that such nations are not so courageous as those that eat flesh. They are pale, a thing not surprising, for the elements of fish must rather repair the lymph than the blood.

Among *ichthyophages*, remarkable instances of longevity are observed, either because light food preserves them from plethora, or that the juices it contains being formed by nature only to constitute cartilages which never bears long duration, their use retards the solidification of the parts of the body which, after all, is the cause of death.

Be this as it may, fish in the hands of a skilful cook is an inexhaustible source of enjoyment. It is served up whole, in pieces, truncated with water, oil, vinegar, warm, cold; and is always well received. It is, however never better than when dressed *en matilotte*.

This ragout, though made a necessary dish to the boatmen on our rivers, and made in perfection only by the keepers of cobarets on their banks, is incomparably good. Lovers of fish never see it without expressing their gratification, either on account of its freshness of taste, or because they can without difficulty eat an indefinite quantity, without any fear of satiety or indigestion. Analytical gastronomy has sought to ascertain what are the effects of a fish diet on the animal system. Unanimous observation leads us to think that it has great influence on the genesiac sense, and awakens the instinct of reproduction in the two sexes. This effect being once known, two causes were at once assigned for it:

1st. The different manner of preparing fish, all the seasoning for it being irritating, such as carar, hering, *thon mariné*, etc.

2d. The various juices the fish imbibes, which are highly inflammable and oxigenise in digestion.

Profound analysis has discovered a yet more powerful cause: the presence of phosphorous in all the portions, and which decomposition soon developes.

These physical truths were doubtlesis unknown to the ecclesiastical legislators, who imposed the lenten diet on different communities of monks, such as Chartreux, Recollets, Trappists, and the Carmelites reformed by Saint Theresa; no one thinks that they wished to throw a new difficulty into the way of the observance of the already most anti-social vow of chastity.

In this state of affairs, beyond doubt, glorious victories were won, and rebellious senses were subjected; there were, however, many lapses and defeats. They must have been well averred, for the result was the religious orders had ultimately a reputation like that of Hercules and the daughters of Danaus, or Marshal Saxe with M'lle Lecouvreur.

They might also have been delighted by an anecdote, so old as to date from the crusades.

Sultan Saladin being anxious to measure the continence of devises, took two into his palace, and for a long time fed them on the most succulent food.

Soon all traces of fasting began to disappear, and they reached a very comfortable *embonpoint*. At that time they were given as companions two *odalisques* of great beauty, all of whose well- directed attacks failed, and they came from the ordeal pure as the diamond of Visapor.

The Sultan kept them in his palace, and to celebrate their triumph fed them for several weeks on fish alone.

After a few days they were again submitted to the ordeal of the odalisques, and.........

In the present state of our knowledge, it is probable that if the course of events were to establish any monastic order, the superiors would adopt some regimen better calculated to maintain its objects.

PHILOSOPHICAL REFLECTION

Fish, considered in general, is an inexhaustible source of reflection to the philosopher.

The varied forms of these strange animals, the senses they are deprived of, and the limited nature of those they have, their various modes of existence, the influence exerted over them by the medium in which they live, move, and breathe, extend the range of our ideas and the indefinite modifications which result from their nature, motions and lives.

For my part, I entertain to them a sentiment very like respect, resulting from my belief that they belong to antediluvian races. The great convulsion which doomed our ancestors, in the eighteenth century of the world, to fish was a season of joy, triumph and festivity.

Section VII. TRUFFLES

Who ever says truffle, pronounces a great word, which awakens eratic and gourmand ideas both in the sex dressed in petticoats and in the bearded portion of humanity.

This honorable duplication results from the fact that the tubercle is not only delicious to the taste, but that it excites a power the exercise of which is accompanied by the most delicious pleasures.

The origin of the truffle is unknown; they are found, but none know how they vegetate. The most learned men have sought to ascertain the secret, and fancied they discovered the seed. Their promises, however, were vain, and no planting was ever followed by a harvest. This perhaps is all right, for as one of the great values of truffles is their dearness, perhaps they would be less highly esteemed if they were cheaper.

"Rejoice, my friend," said I, "a superb lace is about to be manufactured at a very low price."

"Ah!" replied she, "think you, if it be cheap, that any one would wear it?"

ERATIC VIRTUE OF TRUFFLES

The Romans were well acquainted with the truffle, but I do not think they were acquainted with the French variety. Those which were their delight were obtained from Greece and Africa, and especially from Libia. The substance was pale, tinged with rose, and the Libian truffles were sought for as being far the most delicate and highly perfumed.

"Gustus elementa per omnia quaerunt."
JUVENAL

From the Romans to our own time, there was a long interregnum, and the resurrection of truffles is an event of recent occurrence. I have read many old books, in which there is no allusion to them. The generation for which I write may almost be said to witness its resurrection.

About 1780 truffles were very rare in Paris, and they were to be had only in small quantities at the *Hotel des Americans*, and at the *Hotel de Province*. A dindon truffée was a luxury only seen at the tables of great nobles and of kept women.

We owe their abundance to dealers in comestibles, the number of whom has greatly increased, and who, seeing that their merchandise was popular, had it sought for throughout the kingdom. Sending for it by either the mail or by couriers, they made its search general. As truffles cannot be planted, careful search alone can obtain it.

At the time I write (1825) the glory of the truffle is at its apogee. Let no one ever confess that he dined where truffles were not. However good any entree may be, it seems bad unless enriched by truffles. Who has not felt his mouth water when any allusion was made to truffles *a la provinçale.*

A sauté of truffles is a dish the honors of which the mistress of the house reserves to herself; in fine, the truffle is the diamond of the kitchen.

I sought the reason of this preference; it seemed to me that many other substances had an equal right to the honor, and I became satisfied that the cause was that the truffle was supposed to excite the genesiac sense. This I am sure is the chief quality of its perfection, and the predilection and preference evinced for it, so powerful is our servitude to this tyrannical and capricious sense.

This discovery led me to seek to ascertain if the effect were real or imaginary.

[The Translator here has thought it best to omit a very BROAD dialogue, which Brillat-Savarin introduced into his book.]

.... I made ulterior researches, collected my ideas, and consulted the men who were most likely to know, with all of whom I was intimate. I united them into a tribunal, a senate, a sanhedrim, an areopagus, and we gave the following decision to be commented upon by the *litterateures* of the twenty-eighth century.

"The truffle is a positive aphrodisiac, and under certain circumstances makes women kinder, and men more amiable."

In Piedmont white truffles are met with, which are very highly esteemed. They have a slight flavor, not injurious to their perfection, because it gives no disagreable return.

The best truffles of France come from Perigord, and upper Provence. About the month of January they have their highest perfume.

Those from Bugey also have a high flavor, but can not be preserved.

Those of Burgundy and Dauphiny are of inferior quality. They are hard, and are deficient in farinacious matter. Thus, there are many kinds of truffles.

To find truffles, dogs and hogs are used, that have been trained to the purpose. There are men, however, with such practised eyes that by the inspection of the soil they can say whether it contains truffles or not, and what is their quality.

ARE TRUFFLES INDIGESTIBLES?

We have only to ascertain if the truffle be indigestible or not.

We say no.

This decision is *ex cathedrâ*, and well sustained.

1. By the nature of the substance. The truffle is easily masticated, is light, and has nothing hard nor cartilaginous in its composition.

2. During our observations for fifty years, we have never known any indigestion to result from truffles.[20]

3. The attestation of the most eminent of the faculty of Paris, a city eminently *gourmande* and trufflivorous, sustains this idea.

4. From the daily conduct of the doctors of the law, who, *cæteris paribus*, consume more truffles than any other class of citizens. Doctor Malonet used to eat enough to give an elephant the indigestion. He however lived to be eighty-six.

We may therefore look on it as certain, that the truffle is a food healthy as it is agreeable, and that when taken in moderation it passes through the system as a letter does through the post office.

One may easily be indisposed after a great dinner, where other things than truffles have been eaten; such accidents, however, only happen to those who, after the first service, were already stuffed like canons, and who failed in the second, leaving the luxuries offered them untouched.

This is not then the fault of truffles, and we may be sure they had swallowed so many glasses of pure water or eaten the same number of potatoes.

Let us conclude by a circumstance which shows how easily we may be mistaken without careful observation.

One day I invited Mr. S–, a very pleasant old man, to dine with me. He was also a gourmand of the highest grade. Either because I knew his tastes, or to satisfy all my guests that I wished to make them happy, I was not sparing in truffles, and they appeared under the egis of young turkeys most carefully stuffed.

---

[20] The translator has known several such indigestions. He once nearly became a martyr to a *galatine de Perdrix truffée*, at the restaurant of the late M. Dandurand.

Mr. S–ate with energy, and as I knew he could not injure himself I left him alone, persuading him not to hurry himself because no one would attack the property he had acquired.

All passed off very well, and we separated at a very late hour. When we reached home, however, Mr. S– was attacked by a violent cholic, a disposition to vomit, convulsive cramp, and general indisposition.

This state of things lasted some time, and all said he suffered from the indigestion caused by truffles; at last nature came to the patient's aid, and Mr. S– opened his mouth and threw up a single truffle, which struck the wall and rebounded, luckily without injury to the by-standers.

All unpleasant symptoms at once disappeared, tranquility was restored, digestion recommenced its course, the patient went to sleep and awoke in the morning perfectly well.

The cause was easily understood, Mr. S–had been eating a long time, and his teeth were unable to sustain the labor imposed on them. He had lost many of those precious members, and those he had left did not always meet together.

A truffle had thus escaped mastication, and almost whole had been swallowed. Digestion had carried it to the pylorus where it was momentarily detained, and this mechanical detention had caused all his trouble, as expulsion had cured it.

Thus there was no indigestion, but merely the interposition of a foreign body.

This was decided on by the consulting body, which saw the *corpus delicti*, and which selected me as its reporter.

Mr. S– did not on this account remain a whit less fond of truffles. He always attacked them with the same audacity, but was very careful to swallow them with more prudence. He used to thank God that this sanitary precaution had prolonged his life and his enjoyments.

Section VIII. SUGAR

In the present state of science we understand by sugar a substance mild to the taste, crystalizable, and which by fermentation resolves itself into carbonic acid and alcohol.

By sugar once was understood only the crystalized juice of the cane, (*arundo saccharifera.*)

A few pages of old authors would induce us to think the ancients had observed in certain arundines a sweet and extractible portion. Lucanus says:

"Qui bibunt tenera dulces ab arundine succos."

Between water sweetened by the juice of the cane, and the sugar we have, there is a great difference. Art in Rome was not far enough advanced to accomplish it.

Sugar really originated in the colonies of the New World. The cane was imported thither two centuries ago and prospered, and effort was made to utilize the juice which flowed from it, and by gradual experiments they accomplished the manufacture of all the variety of its productions we know of.

The culture of the sugar cane has become an object of the greatest importance; it is a great source of wealth both to the cultivators and the vendors, and also to the taxes of governments who levy an import on it.

INDIGENOUS SUGAR

It has long been thought that tropical heat was not needed to form sugar. About 1740 Morgroff discovered that many plants of the temperate zones, and among others the beet contained it.

Towards the beginning of the nineteenth century, circumstances having made sugar scarce, and consequently dear, the government made it an object for savants to look for it.

The idea was successful, and it was ascertained that sugar was found in the whole vegetable kingdom; that it existed in the grape, chestnut, potato, and in the beet especially.

This last plant became an object of the greatest culture, and many experiments proved that in this respect, the old world could do without the new. France was covered with manufactories, which worked with different success, and the manufacture of sugar became naturalized; the art was a new one which may any day be recalled.

Among the various manufactories, the most prominent was that established at Passy, near Paris, by Mr. Benjamin Delassert, a citizen, the name of whom is always connected with the good and useful.

By means of a series of extensive operations, he got rid of all that was doubtful in the practice, and made no mystery of his plan of procedure, even to those who were his rivals. He was visited by the head of the government, and was ordered to furnish all that was needed at the Tuilleries.

New circumstances, the restoration of peace, having again reduced colonial sugar to a lower price, the French manufacturers lost the advantages they had gained. Many, however, yet prosper, and Delassert makes some thousands every year. This also enables him to preserve his processes until the time comes when they may again he useful.[21]

When beet sugar was in the market, party men, up-starts and fools, took it into their heads that its flavor was unpleasant, and some even said it was unhealthy.

Many experiments have proved the contrary, and the Count de Chaptal, in his excellent book, Chemistry Applied to Agriculture," (vol. ii. page 13,) says:

"Sugars obtained from various plants, says a celebrated chemist, are in fact of the same nature, and have no intrinsic difference when they are equally pure. Taste, crystalization, color, weight, are absolutely identical, and the most acute observer cannot distinguish the one from the other."

An idea of the force of prejudice is afforded by the fact, that out of one hundred British subjects, taken at random, not ten believe in the possibility of obtaining sugar from the beet.

USES OF SUGAR

Sugar was introduced by the apothecaries. With them it was a most important article, for when a person was greatly in want of any article, there was a proverb, "*Like an apothecary without sugar.*"

To say that it came thence, is to say that it was received with disfavor; some said that it was heating, others that it injured the chest; some that it disposed

---

[21] We may add, that at the session for the general encouragement of national industry, a medal was ordered to be presented to M. Crespel, a manufacturer of arrus, who manufactures every year one hundred and fifty thousand pounds of beet sugar, which he sells at a profit, even—when Colonial sugar is 2 francs 50 centimes the kilogramme. The reason is, that the refuse is used for distillation, and subsequently fed out to cattle.

persons to apoplexy. Calumny, however, had to give way to truth, and for eighty years this apothegm has been current, "Sugar hurts nothing but the purse."

Under this impenetrable aegis the use of sugar has increased every day, and no alimentary substance has undergone so many transformations. Many persons like sugar in a pure state, and in hopeless cases the faculty recommend it as a substance which can do no possible harm, and which is not unpleasant.

Mixed with water, it gives us *eau sucrée*, a refreshing drink, which is healthful, agreeable, and sometimes salutary.

Mingled in large quantities with water it constitutes *sirops*, which are perfumed, and from their variety are most refreshing.

Mingled with water, the caloric of which is artificially extracted, it furnishes two kinds, which are of Italian origin, and were introduced into France by Catharine de Medici.

With wine it furnishes such a restorative power that in some countries roasted meats taken to the bride and groom are covered with it, just as in Persia soused sheep's' feet are given them.

Mingled with flour and eggs, it furnishes biscuits, maccaronies, etc., etc., *ad infinitum*.

With milk it unites in the composition of creams, *blanc-mangers* and other dishes of the second course, substituting for the substantial taste of meat, ethereal perfumes.

It causes the aroma of coffee to be exhaled.

Mingled with *café au lait*, a light, pleasant aliment is produced, precisely suited to those who have to go to their offices immediately after breakfast.

With fruits and flowers it contributes to furnish confitures, marmalades, preserves, pates and candies, and enables us to enjoy the perfume of those flowers long after they have withered.

It may be that sugar might be advantageously employed in embalming, an art of which we know little.

Sugar mingled with alcohol furnishes spirituous liquors, such as were used, it is said, to warm the old blood of Louis XIV., which, by their energy, seized the palate and the taste by the perfumed gas united to them, the two qualities forming the ne plus ultra of the pleasures of the taste.

Such is the substance which the French of the time of Louis XIII. scarcely knew the name of, and which to the people of the nineteenth century is become so important; no woman, in easy circumstances, spends as much money for bread as she does for sugar.

M. Delacroix, a man of letters, who is as industrious as he is profound, was one day complaining of the price of sugar, which then cost five francs a pound, "Ah!" said he, "if sugar should ever again be thirty sous a pound, I will drink nothing but eau sucree." His wishes were granted; he yet lives, and I trust he keeps his word.

Section IX. ORIGIN OF COFFEE

The first coffee tree was found in Arabia, and in spite of the various transplantations it has undergone, the best coffee is yet obtained there. An old tradition states that coffee was discovered by a shepherd of old, who saw that his flock was always in the greatest state of excitement and hilarity when they browsed on the leaves of the coffee tree.

Though this may be but an old story, the honor of the discovery belongs only in part to the goatherd. The rest belongs to him who first made use of the bean, and boiled it.

A mere decoction of green coffee is a most insipid drink, but carbonization develops the aroma and forms an oil which is the peculiarity of the coffee we drink, and which would have been eternally unknown but for the intervention of heat.

The Turks excel us in this. They employ no mill to triturate the coffee, but beat it with wooden pestles in mortars. When the pestles have been long used, they become precious and are sold at great prices.

I had to examine and determine whether in the result one or the other of the two methods be preferable.

Consequently, I burned carefully a pound of good mocha, and separated it into two equal portions, the one of which was passed through the mill, and the other beaten Turkish fashion in a mortar.

I made coffee of each, taking equal weights of each, poured on an equal weight of boiling water and treated them both precisely alike.

I tasted this coffee myself, and caused others who were competent judges to do so. The unanimous opinion was that coffee which had been beaten in a mortar was far better than that which had been ground.

Any one may repeat the experiment. In the interim I will tell you a strange anecdote of the influence of one or the other kind of manipulation.

"Monsieur," said Napoleon, one day to Laplace, "how comes it that a glass of water into which I put a lump of loaf sugar tastes more pleasantly than if I had put in the same quantity of crushed sugar." "Sire," said the philosophic Senator, "there are three substances the constituents of which are identical—Sugar, gum and amidon; they differ only in certain conditions, the secret of which nature has preserved. I think it possible that in the effect produced by the pestle some saccharine particles become either gum or amidon, and cause the difference."

This remark became public, and ulterior observations has confirmed it.

DIFFERENT MODES OF PREPARING COFFEE

Some years ago all directed their attention to the mode of preparing coffee; the reason doubtless was that the head of the government was fond of it.

Some proposed not to burn nor to powder it, to boil it three quarters of an hour, to strain it, &c.

I have tried this and all the methods which have been suggested from day to day, and prefer that known as *a la Dubelloy*, which consists in pouring boiling water on coffee placed in a porcelain or silver vessel pierced with a number of very minute holes. This first decoction should be taken and brought to the boiling point, then passed through the strainer again, and a coffee will be obtained clear and strong as possible.

I have also tried to make coffee in a high pressure boiling apparatus; all I obtained however was a fluid intensely bitter, and strong enough to take the skin from the throat of a Cossack.

EFFECTS OF COFFEE

Doctors have differed in relation to the sanitary properties of coffee. We will omit all this, and devote ourselves to the more important point, its influence on the organs of thought.

There is no doubt but that coffee greatly excites the cerebral faculties. Any man who drinks it for the first time is almost sure to pass a sleepless night.

Sometimes the effect is softened or modified by custom, but there are many persons on whom it always produces this effect, and who consequently cannot use coffee.

I have said that the effect was modified by use, a circumstance which does not prevent its having effect in another manner. I have observed persons whom coffee did not prevent from sleeping at night, need it to keep them awake during the day, and never failed to slumber when they had taken it for dinner. There are others who are torpid all day when they have not taken their cup in the morning.

Voltaire and Buffon used a great deal of coffee. Perchance the latter was indebted to it for the admirable clearness we observe in his works, and the second for the harmonious enthusiasm of his style. It is evident that many pages of the treatise on man, the dog, the tiger, lion and horse, were written under a strange cerebral excitement.

The loss of sleep caused by coffee is not painful, for the perceptions are very clear, and one has no disposition to sleep. One is always excited and unhappy when wakefulness comes from any other cause. This, however, does prevent such an excitement, when carried too far, from being very injurious.

Formerly only persons of mature age took coffee. Now every one takes it, and perhaps it is the taste which forces onward the immense crowd that besiege all the avenues of the Olympus, and of the temple of memory.

The Cordwainer, author of the tragedy of Zenobia, which all Paris heard read a few years ago, drank much coffee; for that reason he excelled the cabinetmaker of Nevers, who was but a drunkard.

Coffee is a more powerful fluid than people generally think. A man in good health may drink two bottles of wine a day for a long time, and sustain his strength. If he drank that quantity of coffee he would become imbecile and die of consumption. I saw at Leicester square, in London, a man whom coffee had made a cripple. He had ceased to suffer, and then drank but six cups a day.

All fathers and mothers should make their children abstain from coffee, if they do not wish them at twenty to be puny dried up machines. People in large cities should pay especial attention to this, as their children have no exaggeration of strength and health, and are not so hearty as those born in the country.

I am one of those who have been obliged to give up coffee, and I will conclude this article by telling how rigorously I was subjected to its power.

The Duke of Mossa, then minister of justice, called on me for an opinion about which I wished to be careful, and for which he had allowed me but a very short time.

I determined then to sit up all night, and to enable me to do so took two large cups of strong and highly flavored coffee.

I went home at seven o'clock to get the papers which had been promised me, but found a note telling me I would not get them until the next day.

Thus in every respect disappointed, I returned to the house where I had dined, and played a game of piquet, without any of the moody fits to which I was ordinarily subject.

I did justice to the coffee, but I was not at ease as to how I would pass the night.

I went to bed at my usual hour, thinking that if I did not get my usual allowance, I would at least get four or five hours, sufficient to carry me through the day.

I was mistaken. I had been two hours in bed and was wider awake than ever; I was in intense mental agitation, and fancied my brain a mill, the wheels of which revolved, grinding nothing.

The idea came to me to turn this fancy to account, and I did so, amusing myself by putting into verse a story I had previously read in an English paper.

I did so without difficulty, and as I did not sleep I undertook another, but in vain. A dozen verses had exhausted my poetic faculty, and I gave it up.

I passed the night without sleep, and without even being stupified for a moment, I arose and passed the day in the same manner. When on the next night I went to bed at my usual hour I made a calculation, and found out that I had not slept for forty hours.

Section X. CHOCOLATE–ITS ORIGIN

The first visiters of America were impelled by a thirst of gold. At that time nothing was appreciated but the products of the mines. Agriculture and commerce were in their infancy, and political economy was as yet unborn. The Spaniards found then the precious metals, an almost sterile discovery, for they decreased in value as they became more abundant. We have other and better ways to increase wealth.

In those regions, however, where a genial sun confers immense fruitfulness on the soil, the cultivation of sugar and coffee was found advantageous. The potato, indigo, vanilla, guano, cocoa, were also discovered; these are its real treasures.

If these discoveries took place in spite of the barriers opposed to curiosity by a jealous nation, we may reasonably hope that they will be multiplied ten-fold in the course of the years to come; and that the explorations of the savants of old Europe will enrich the three kingdoms with a multitude of substances which will give us new sensations, as vanilla has, or augment our alimentary resources, as cocoa.

It has been determined to call chocolate the result of the paste of cocoa burnt with sugar and the bark of the cinnamon. This is the technical definition of chocolate. Sugar is the integral part, for without sugar the compound is cocoa and, chocolate. To sugar, cinnamon and cocoa is joined the delicious aroma of vanilla, and thus is obtained the *ne plus ultra* to which this preparation can be carried.

To this small number of ingredients has been reduced the number of things sought to mingle with cocoa in the manufacture of chocolate. Pepper, pimento, anise seed, ginger and others, have necessarily been tried.

The cocoa tree is a native of South America, and is found both in the islands and on the continent. It has been confessed, however, that the best fruit is produced by the trees which grow on the banks of Moracaibo, in the valleys of Caracas, and in the province of Sokomusko. The fruit is larger, the sugar less bitter, and the taste higher. Since these regions have become accessible, a comparison may be made every day and the palate will never be deceived.

The Spanish women of the new world are passionately fond of chocolate; and not satisfied with taking it two or three times a day, have it even sent after them to church. This sensuality has often drawn down the censure of their bishops, who, however, gradually closed their eyes to it. The reverend father Escobar, the metaphysics of whom was subtle as his morals were accommodating, used to declare that chocolate made with water did not break a fast; thus for the use of his penitents reproducing the old adage, "*Liquidum non frangit jejunium.*"

Chocolate was brought to Spain about the end of the seventeenth century, and the use became at once common. Women especially showed great fondness for it. Manners have not changed in this particular as yet, and now throughout all the peninsula chocolate is presented on all occasions when it is usual to offer any refreshment.

Chocolate crossed the mountains with Anne of Austria, the daughter of Philip II., and wife of Louis XIII. The Spanish monks also made it known, by presents to their brethren in France. The Spanish ambassadors also made it popular, and during the regency it was more universally used than coffee, because it was taken as an agreeable food, while coffee was esteemed a luxury.

Linnaeus calls the cocoa *cacao theobroma*, (cocoa, the drink of the gods). A cause for this name has been sought. Some assign his passionate fondness for it, and the other his desire to please his confessor; there are those who attribute it to gallantry, a Queen having first introduced it. (*Incertum.*)

PROPERTIES OF CHOCOLATE

Chocolate has given occasion to profound dissertations, with the object of determining its nature and properties, and to place it in the category of warm, cold, or temperate drinks. We must own all their lucubrations have contributed but slightly to the elucidation of truth.

It was left for time and experience, those two great masters, to show that chocolate prepared with care is as healthful as it is agreeable. That it is nourishing, easily digested, and is not so injurious to beauty as coffee said to be. It is very suitable to persons who have much mental toil, to professors and lawyers, especially to lawyers. It also suits certain feeble stomachs, and has been thought most advantageous in chronic diseases. It is the last resource in affections of the *pylorus*.

These various properties chocolate owes to nothing but an *eloesaccharum*. Few substances contain in the same volume more nutrition. It becomes almost entirely animalised.

During the war, cocoa was rare and very dear. Substitutes were sought for, but all efforts were vain. One of the blessings of peace was that it rid us of all those humbugs one was forced to taste, but which were no more chocolate than chicory is mocha.

Some persons complain that they cannot digest chocolate. Others say that it does not nourish them, and that it passes away too quickly.

The probability is that the first have only to blame themselves, and that the chocolate they use is of bad quality. Even the weakest stomach can digest good and well-made chocolate.

The others have an easy remedy, and they need only strengthen their stomachs by a *pâté*, a *côtelette*, or a jerked kidney. Then let them take a bowl of sokomusko, and thank God for such a powerful stomach.

Here I have an opportunity to give two examples, the correctness of which may be relied on.

After a good breakfast one may drink a full bowl of chocolate, and digestion in three hours will be perfect, so that one may dine at any hour that is pleasant. ... In zeal for the advancement of the science, I tried this experiment on many ladies who assured me they would die. They did not, though, and lived to glorify the professor.

Those who use chocolate, ordinarily enjoy the most perfect health, and are the least subject to the multitude of ailments which destroy life; their embonpoint is stationary. These two examples any one can verify in society by a scrutiny of those the regimen of whom is known.

This is the true place to speak of the properties of chocolate, which I have verified by many examples and experiments, which I am delighted to exhibit to my readers. (*See varieties at the end of the volume.*)

Now, then, let any man who has indulged too much in the cup of *volupté*; let every man who has passed in toil too much of the time when he should have slept; let every man of mind, who finds his faculties temporarily decay; every man who finds the air humid and the atmosphere painful to breathe; let every man who has a fixed idea which would deprive him of the liberty of thought; let them each take a *demi litre* of *chocolate ambré*, (sixty grains of amber to the kilogramme), and they will see wonders.

In my way of distinguishing things, I have called this *chocolate des affligés*; because in all the conditions I have referred to, there is something very like affliction.

Very good chocolate is made in Spain; one is indisposed to send thither for it, for all manufacturers are not equally skillful, and when it comes it has to be used as it is.

Italian chocolates do not suit the French, for the cocoa is burned too much. This makes the chocolate bitter, and deprives it of its nourishment. A portion of the bean has been reduced to carbon.

Chocolate having become common in France, all sought to learn how to make it. Few, however, approximated to perfection for the art is not easy.

In the first place it was necessary to know good cocoa and to use it in all its purity. There is no first quality case that has not its inferiorities, and a mistaken interest often causes damaged beans to be put in, which should have been rejected. The roasting of the cocoa is also a delicate operation, and requires a tact very like inspiration. Some have the faculty naturally, and are never mistaken.

A peculiar talent is necessary to regulate the quantity of sugar which enters into the composition. It is not invariable and a matter of course, but varies in proportion to the aroma of the bean and the degree of torrefaction.

The trituration and mixture do not demand less care, and on them depends the greater or less digestibility of chocolate.

Other considerations should also preside over the choice and quantity of aromas, which should not be the same with chocolate made for food and those taken as luxuries. It should also be varied according if the mass is intended to receive vanilla or not. In fine, to make good chocolate a number of very subtle equations must be resolved, and which we take advantage of without suspecting that they ever took place.

For a long time machines have been employed for the manufacture of chocolate. We think this does not add at all to its perfection, but it diminishes manipulation very materially, so that those who have adopted it should be able to sell chocolate at a very low rate.[22] They, however, usually sell it more dearly, and this fact demonstrates that the true spirit of commerce has not yet entered France; the use of machines should be as advantageous to the consumer as to the producer.

---

[22] One of those machines is now in operation in a window in Broadway, New York. It is a model of mechanical appropriateness.

TRUE METHOD OF PREPARING CHOCOLATE

The Americans[23] make their chocolate without sugar. When they wish to take chocolate, they send for chocolate. Every one throws into his cup as much cocoa as it needs, pours warm water in, and adds the sugar and perfumes he wishes.

This method neither suits our habits nor our tastes, for we wish chocolate to come to us ready prepared.

In this state, transcendental chemistry has taught us that it should neither be rasped with the knife nor bruised with a pestle, because thus a portion of the sugar is converted into starch, and the drink made less attractive.

Thus to make chocolate, that is to say, to make it fit for immediate use, about an ounce and a half should be taken for each cup, which should be slowly dissolved in water while it is heated, and stirred from time to time with a spatula of wood. It should be boiled a quarter of an hour, in order to give it consistency, and served up hot.

"Monsieur," said madame d'Arestrel, fifty years ago, to me at Belley, "when you wish good chocolate make it the evening before in a tin pot. The rest of the night gives it a velvet-like flavor that makes it far better. God will not be offended at this little refinement, for in himself is all excellence."

---

[23] South Americans.–TRANSLATOR.

MEDITATION VII

THEORY OF FRYING

It was a fine morning in May; the sun shed his brightest rays on the smoky roofs of the city of enjoyments, and the streets (strangely enough) were filled neither with mud nor dust.

The heavy diligences had long ceased to shake the streets; the heavy wagons had ceased to pass, and only open carriages were seen, in which indigenous and exotic beauties under beautiful hats, cast disdainful looks on ugly, and smiling ones on good- looking cavaliers.

It was three o'clock when the professor sought his armchair to meditate.

His right leg rested vertically on the floor, his left formed a diagonal angle with, and rested on it. His back was comfortably supported, and his hands rested on the lions' heads which terminated the arms of the venerable piece of furniture in which he sat.

His lofty brow indicated intense study, and his mouth a taste for pleasant amusement. His air was collected, and any one to have seen him would have said, "that is a sage of ancient days." The professor sent for his *preparateur en chef*, (chief COOK) and that officer arrived, ready to receive orders, advice or lessons.

ALLOCUTION

"Master la Planche," said the professor with that deep grave accent which penetrates the very depth of our hearts, "all who sit at my table pronounce your *potages* of the first class, a very excellent thing, for potage is the first consolation of an empty stomach. I am sorry to say though that you are uncertain as a *friturier*.[24]

"I heard you sigh yesterday over that magnificent *sole* you served to us, pale, watery and colorless. My friend R.[25] looked disapprovingly of it, M.H.R. turned his

---

[24] *Anglice*. Fryer.
[25] Footnote: Mr. R– -, born at Seyssel, in the district of Belley, in 1757, an elector of the grand college. He may be considered an example of the good effects of prudence and probity.

gastronomical nose to the left, and the President S. declared such a misfortune equal to a public calamity.

"This happened because you neglected the theory, the importance of which you are aware of. You are rather obstinate, though I have, taken the trouble to impress on you the facts, that the operations of your laboratory are only the execution of the eternal laws of nature, and that certain things which you do carelessly, because you have seen others do so; yet these are the results of the highest science. Listen to me, therefore, with attention, that you may never again blush at your works."

Section 1. CHEMISTRY

"Liquids which you subject to the action of fire cannot all receive the same quantity of heat. Nature has formed them differently, and this secret, which we will call CAPACITY FOR CALORIC, she has kept to herself.

"You may, therefore, with impunity dip your finger in boiling spirits of wine; you would take it very quickly from boiling brandy; more rapidly yet from water; while the most rapid immersion in boiling oil would heat you easily.

"Consequently warm fluids act differently on the sapid bodies presented to them. Those subject to water soften, dissolve, and reduce themselves to *boilli*. The result is *bouillon* and its extracts. Those on the contrary treated with oil harden, assume a color more or less deep, and finally are carbonized.

"In the first instance, water dissolves and conveys away the interior juices of the alimentary substances placed in it. In the second the juices are preserved, for they are insoluble in oil. If these things dry up it is because a continuous heat vaporizes the humid parts.

"The two methods have different names, and FRYING is BOILING in oil or grease substances intended to be eaten. I think I have told you that officially oil and grease are synonymous; heating the latter being but a concrete oil."

Section II. APPLICATION

"*Fritures* are well received in entertainments into which they introduce an agreeable variety. They are agreeable to the taste, preserve their primitive flavor, and may be eaten with the hand, a thing women are always fond of.

"Thus cooks are able to hide many things that have appeared on the day before, and remedy unforeseen requisitions on them. It takes no longer to fry a four-pound chop than it does to boil an egg.

"All the merit of the *friture* is derived from the *surprise*, or the invasion of the boiling liquid which carbonizes or burns at the very instant of immersion of the body placed in it.

"To effect a purpose, the liquid must be hot enough to act instantaneously. It does not, however, reach S this point until it has long been submitted to the action of a blazing and hot fire.

"By the following means it may be ascertained if the *friture* be heated to the wished-for degree, cut a piece of bread in the form of a cube, and dip it in the pan for five or six seconds, if you take it out firm and dark put in what you wish to prepare immediately. If it be not, stir the fire and begin again.

"The surprise being once effected, moderate the fire that the action may not be too hurried, and that by a prolonged heat the juices it contains may be changed and the flavor enhanced.

"You have doubtless observed that *fritures* dissolve neither the sugar nor salt their respective natures require. You should not fail then to reduce those substances to a very fine powder in order that they may adhere the more readily, and season the dish by juxtaposition.

"I do not tell you about oils and greases for the different treatises I have put in your library give you sufficient light.

"Do not forget, however, when you get one of those trout which do not weigh more than half a pound, and which come from murmuring streams, far from the capitol, to use the finest olive oil. This delicate dish duly powdered and garnished with slices of lemon is fit for a cardinal.[26]

"*Eperlans* (smelt or sprat) should be treated in the same manner. This is the *becfique* of the water, and has the same perfume and excellence.

-----

[26] Mr. Aulissin, a very well informed Neapolitan lawyer, and a good amateur performer on the violoncello, dining one day with me, and eating some thing that pleased him, said–"*Questo e un vero boccone di cardinale.*" "Why," said I, in the same tongue, not say "*boccone in Ré.*" "Seignore," said he, "we Italians do nothing; a king cannot be a gourmand, for royal dinners are too short and solemn. With cardinals things are very different." He shrugged his shoulders as he spoke.

"These two prescriptions are founded in the very nature of things. Experience tells us that olive oil should only be used with things which are soon cooked, and which do not demand too high a temperature, because prolonged ebullition developes an empyreumatic and disagreable taste produced by a few particles of pulp, which can, being impossible to be gotten rid of, carbonize.

"You tried my furnace, and were the first person who ever succeeded in producing an immense fried turbot. On that day there was great rejoicing among the elect.

"Continue to be coeval in all you attempt, and never forget that from the moment guests enter the salon WE are responsible for their happiness."

MEDITATION VIII

ON THIRST

THIRST is the internal feeling of a wish to drink.

A heat of about 32 [degrees] Réaumur, constantly vaporizing the different fluids the circulation of which sustains life, the diminution they undergo would unfit them for their purposes, if they were not renewed and refreshed. The necessity of this renewal is what we call thirst.

We think the seat of thirst is in the digestive system. When athirst (we have often felt the sensation when hunting) we feel distinctly that all the inhaling portions of the nostrils, mouth and throat are benumbed and hardened, and that if thirst be sometimes appeased by the application of fluids to other parts of the body, as in the bath, the reason is that as soon as they are absorbed they hurry rapidly to the seat of the evil and become remedies.

VARIETIES OF THIRST

Looking at the subject in all its bearings we may count three varieties of thirst: latent, factitious and permanent.

Latent or habitual thirst, is the insensible equilibrium established between transpiratory vaporization and the necessity of supplying what is lost. Thus, though we experience no pain, we are invited to drink while we eat, and are able to drink at almost every moment of the day. This thirst accompanies us everywhere, and is almost a portion of our existence.

Factitious thirst is peculiar to man, and results from the instinct which impels him to seek in drink the strength he needs. It is an artificial enjoyment rather than a natural want. This thirst is really governless, because the fluids we take have the faculty of reviving it, and this thirst becomes habitual, makes drunkards in every country. The consequence is, that they drink as long as liquor lasts, or until they are utterly overcome.

When, on the other hand, thirst is appeased by pure water, which seems the most natural remedy, we never drink more than we actually need.

Hardening thirst is the result of the increase of the want, and of the impossibility to satisfy latent thirst.

It is so called because it is accompanied by hardness of the tongue, dryness of the palate, and a devouring heat in all the body.

The sensation of thirst is so intense, that in all tongues it is synonymous with excessive desire, and irrepressible longing: thus we thirst for gold, wealth, power, science, &c., expressions which never would have become common had men not have been athirst and aware of their vengeance.

Appetite is pleasant when it does not reach the point of hunger. Thirst is not so, and as soon as we feel it we are uncomfortable and anxious. When there is no possibility of appeasing it, the state of mind is terrible.

To compensate us for this, the sense of thirst procures us great pleasure; and when great thirst is appeased, or a delicious drink is offered to one moderately athirst, the whole papillary system is aroused, from the tip of the tongue to the extremity of the stomach.

We die of thirst more rapidly than of hunger. Men with an abundance of water, have lived for eight days without bread. Without water, the system succumbs on the fifth.

The reason is that in starving, man dies more of weakness; in thirst of a burning fever.

People are not always able to resist thirst so long: in 1787, one of the hundred Swiss of Louis XVI., died from having been twenty- four hours without drink.

He was at a cabaret with some of his comrades, and as he was about to carry his glass to his lips, he was reproached with drinking oftener than the rest, and with not being able to do a moment without it.

He then made a bet of ten bottles of wine, that he would not drink for twenty-four hours.

He ceased at once, and sat by, for two hours, seeing the others drink.

The night passed well enough, but at dawn he found it difficult to do without his habitual glass of brandy.

All the morning he was uneasy and troubled; he went hither and thither without reason, and seemed not to know what he was about.

At one o'clock he laid down, fancying he would be calmer: he was really sick, but those about him could not induce him to drink. He said he could get on till evening: he wished to gain his bet, and it is probable also, that some military pride was mingled in the matter, which prevented him from yielding to pain.

He kept up until seven o'clock, but at half-after seven was very sick and soon died, without being able to swallow a glass of wine which was presented to him.

I was informed of all these details that very night, by the Sieur Schneider, the fifer of the hundred Swiss, in the house of whom I lived at Versailles.

CAUSES OF THIRST

Many circumstances, either united or separate, contribute to thirst. We shall mention some which are not without influence on our habits.

Heat augments thirst. Whence comes the disposition men have always had to build their habitations near the sea.

Corporeal labor augments thirst. Persons who employ labourers, always gratify them by drink—hence the proverb that wine given them is always well sold.

Dancing increases thirst, and for this reason the ball-room is always supplied with invigorating drinks.

Declamation also increases thirst, which accounts for the glass of water readers always seek to drink with grace, and which is always beside the white handkerchief on the desk.

Genesiac pleasure excites thirst, and accounts for the poetical descriptions of Cyprus, Amathonte, Gnidus, and other homes of Venus, in which there are always shady groves and murmuring streamlets.

Song augments thirst, and therefore all vocalists are said to be such huge drinkers. A musician myself, I protest against this assertion, which has neither rhyme nor reason.

The artists in our saloons drink with as much prudence as sagacity; what they lose in this, however, they atone for on the other side; if not given to drink, they are untiring gourmands, so much so, that I am told at the Circle of Transcendental Harmony,[27] the festivals of St. Cecile lasted twenty-four hours.

---

[27] A well-known "Musical Society."

EXAMPLE

Exposure to a rapid current of air, causes a rapid augmentation of thirst, and I think the following observations will be read with pleasure by all the lovers of the chase.

It is well known that quail are fond of huge mountains, where their broods are in more safety, from the fact that the harvests are later.

When the rye is cut, they go into the barley and oats; and when the latter is being harvested, they go into that portion which is less matured.

This is the time to shoot them; because in a small number of acres, are found all the birds which a few months before were strewn through a whole commune and are at that time fat as possible.

I went with some friends for the purpose of shooting to a mountain in the *arrondissiment* of Nantua, in the canton known as *plan d'Hotonne*, where we were about to commence the day's work under a brighter sun than any Parisian *badaud* ever saw.

While we were at breakfast a violent north wind arose which was much in the way of our sport: we however continued.

We had scarcely been out a quarter of an hour, when the most effeminate of the party said he was thirsty. We now, doubtless, would have laughed at him, had we not all experienced the same sensation.

We all drank, for an ass loaded with refreshments followed us, but the relief afforded was of brief duration. The thirst soon appeared with increased intensity, so that some fancied themselves sick, and others were becoming so, and all talked of returning. To do so was to have travelled ten leagues for no purpose.

I had time to collect my ideas, and saw the reason of this strange thirst; and told them we suffered from the effects of three causes. The dimunition of atmospheric pressure made our circulation more rapid. The sun heated us, and walking had increased transpiration. More than all these—the wind dried up this transpiration, and prevented all moistness of the skin.

I told them that there was no danger, that the enemy was known, and that we must oppose it.

Precaution however was ineffectual, for their thirst was quenchless. Water, wine and water, and brandy, all were powerless. We suffered from thirst even while we drank, and were uncomfortable all day.

We got through the day, however; the owner of the domain of Latour entertaining us, joining the provisions we had, to his own stores.

We dined very well and got into the hay-loft, where we slept soundly.

The next day's experience showed my theory to be true. The wind lulled, the sun was not so warm, and we experienced no inconvenience from thirst.

But a great misfortune had befallen us. We had very prudently filled our canteens, but they had not been able to resist the many assaults made on them. They were bodies without souls, and we all fell into the hands of the *cabaret-keepers*.

We had to come to that point, not however without murmuring. I addressed an allocution full of reproaches to the wind, when I saw a dish fit to be set before a king, "*D'epinards a la graisse de cailles*," destined to be eaten with a wine scarcely as good as that of Surène.[28]

---

[28] A village two leagues from Paris, famous for its bad wine. There is a proverb which says that to get rid of a glass of Surene, three things are needed, "a drinker and two men to hold him in case his courage fails." The same may be said of Perieux, which people however will drink.

MEDITATION IX

ON DRINKS. [29]

By drinks we mean all liquids which mingle with food.

Water seems to be the natural drink. Wherever there is animal life it is found, and replaces milk. For adults it is as necessary as air.

WATER

Water is the only fluid which really appeases thirst, and for that reason only a small quantity of it can be drunk. The majority of other fluids that man drinks are only palliatives, and had he drunk nothing else he never would have said that he drunk without being thirsty.

QUICK EFFECT OF DRINKS

Drinks are absorbed by the animal economy with the most extreme facility. Their effect is prompt and the relief they furnish is almost instantaneous. Give the most hungry man you can meet with the richest possible food, he will eat with difficulty. Give him a glass of wine or of brandy, and at once he will find himself better.

I can establish this theory by a very remarkable circumstance I received from my nephew, Colonel Guigard, a man not disposed to tell long stories. All may rely upon the accuracy of what he has said.

He was at the head of a detachment returning from the siege of Jaffa, and was but a few hundred paces from the place where he expected to find water, and where he met many of the advanced guard already dead with heat.

Among the victims of this burning climate was a *carabinier* who was known to many persons of the detachment.

---

[29] This chapter is purely philosophical: a description of different kinds of wine does not enter into the plan I have marked out for myself. If it was, I would never have finished my book.

Many of his comrades who approached him for the last time, either to inherit what he had left, or to bid him adieu, were amazed to find his limbs flexible and something flexible around his heart.

"Give him a drop of *sacré chien*" said the *lustig* of the troupe. "If he is not too far gone into the other world, he will come back to taste it."

At the reception of the first spoonful of spirits he opened his eyes: they then rubbed his temples and gave him a drop or two. After about an hour he was able to sit up in the saddle.

He was taken to a fountain, nursed during the night, and carefully attended to. On the next day he reached Cairo.

STRONG DRINKS

There is one thing very worthy of attention; the instinct which leads us to look for intoxicating drinks.

Wine, the most pleasant of all drinks, whether due to Noah who planted the vine, or to Bacchus who expressed the juice of the grape, dates back to the infancy of the world. Beer, which is attributed to Osiris, dates to an age far beyond history.

All men, even those we call savages, have been so tormented by the passion for strong drinks, that limited as their capacities were, they were yet able to manufacture them.

They made the milk of their domestic animals sour: they extracted the juice of many animals and many fruits in which they suspected the idea of fermentation to exist. Wherever men are found, strong liquors are met with, and are used in festivities, sacrifices, marriages, funeral rites, and on all solemn occasions.

For many centuries wine was drank and sung before any persons had an idea that it was possible to extract the spirituous portion, which is the essence of its power. The Arabs, however, taught us the art of distillation, invented by them to extract the perfume of flowers, and especially of the rose, so celebrated in their poems. Then persons began to fancy that in wine a source of excitement might be found to give taste a peculiar exaltation. By gradual experiments alcohol, spirits of wine, and brandy were discovered.

Alcohol is the monarch of liquids, and takes possession of the extreme tastes of the palate. Its various preparations offer us countless new flavors, and to certain medicinal remedies, it gives an energy they could not well do without. It has even become a formidable weapon: the natives of the new world having been more utterly destroyed by brandy than by gunpowder.

The method by which alcohol was discovered, has led to yet more important results, as it consisted in the separation and exhibition of the constituent parts of a body, it became a guide to those engaged in analogous pursuits, and made us acquainted with new substances, such as quinine, morphine, strychnine and other similar ones.

Be this as it may, the thirst for a liquid which nature has shrouded in veils, the extraordinary appetite acting on all races of men, under all climates and temperatures, is well calculated to attract the attention of the observer.

I have often been inclined to place the passion for spirituous liquors, utterly unknown to animals, side by side with anxiety for the future, equally strange to them, and to look on the one and the other as distinctive attributes of the last sublunary revolution.

MEDITATION X

AN EPISODE ON THE END OF THE WORLD

I said–*last sublunary revolution*, and this idea awakened many strange ideas.

Many things demonstrate to us that our globe has undergone many changes, each of which was, so to say, "an end of the world." Some instinct tells us many other changes are to follow.

More than once, we have thought these revolutions likely to come, and the comet of Jerome Lalande has sent many persons to the confessional.

The effect of all this has been that every one is disposed to surround this catastrophe with vengeance, exterminating angels, trumps and other accessories.

Alas! there is no use to take so much trouble to ruin us. We are not worth so much display, and if God please, he can change the surface of the globe without any trouble.

Let us for a moment suppose that one of those wandering stars, the route and mission of which none know, and the appearance of which is always accompanied by some traditional terror; let us suppose that it passes near enough to the sun, to be charged with a superabundance of caloric, and approach near enough to us to create a heat of sixty degrees Reaumur over the whole earth (as hot again as the temperature caused by the comet of 1811.)

All vegetation would die, all sounds would cease. The earth would revolve in silence until other circumstances had evolved other germs: yet the cause of this disaster would have remained lost in the vast fields of air, and would never have approached us nearer than some millions of leagues.

This event, which in the main, has ever seemed to me a fit subject for reverie, and I never ceased for a moment to dwell on it.

This ascending heat is curious to be looked after, and it is not uninteresting to follow its effects, expansion, action, and to ask:

How great it was during the first, second, and subsequent days.

What effect it had on the earth, and water, and on the formation and mingling, and detonation of gasses.

What influence it had on men, as far as age, sex, strength and weakness are concerned.

What influence it has on obedience to the laws, submission to authority, and respect to persons and property.

What one should do to escape from danger.

What influence it has on love, friendship, parental affection, self-love and devotion.

What is its influence on the religious sentiments, faith, resignation and hope.

History can furnish us a few facts on its moral influence, for the end of the world has more than once been predicted and determined.

I am very sorry that I cannot tell my readers how I settled all this, but I will not rob them of the pleasure of thinking of the matter themselves. This may somewhat shorten some of their sleepless hours, and ensure them a few *siestas* during the day.

Great danger dissolves all bonds. When the yellow fever was in Philadelphia, in 1792, husbands closed the doors on their wives, children deserted their fathers, and many similar phenomena occurred.

Quod a nobis Deus avertat!

MEDITATION XI

ON GOURMANDISE

I HAVE looked through various dictionaries for the word gourmandise and have found no translation that suited me. It is described as a sort of confusion of gluttony and voracity. Whence I have concluded that lexicographers, though very pleasant people in other respects, are not the sort of men to swallow a partridge wing gracefully with one hand, with a glass of *Laffitte* or *clos de Vougeot* in the other.

They were completely oblivious of social gourmandise, which unites Athenian elegance, Roman luxury and French delicacy; which arranges wisely, flavors energetically, and judges profoundly. This is a precious quality which might be a virtue and which is certainly the source of many pure enjoyments.

DEFINITIONS

Let us understand each other.

Gourmandise is a passionate preference, well determined and satisfied, for objects which flatter our taste.

Gourmandise is hostile to all excesses: any man who becomes drunk or suffers from indigestion is likely to be expunged from the lists.

Gourmandise also comprehends, *friandise* (passion for light delicacies) for pastry, comfitures, etc. This is a modification introduced for the special benefit of women, and men like the other sex.

Look at gourmandise under any aspect you please, and it deserves praise.

Physically, it is a demonstration of the healthy state of the organs of nutrition.

Morally, it is implicit resignation to the orders of God, who made us eat to live, invites us to do so by appetite, sustains us by flavor, and rewards us by pleasure.

ADVANTAGES OF GOURMANDISE

Considered from the points of view of political economy, gourmandise is the common bond which unites the people in reciprocal exchanges of the articles needed for daily consumption.

This is the cause of voyages from one pole to the other, for brandy, spices, sugars, seasonings and provisions of every kind, even eggs and melons.

This it is which gives a proportional price to things, either *mediocres*, good or excellent, whether the articles derive them out of, or from nature.

This it is that sustains the emulation of the crowd of fishermen, huntsmen, gardeners and others, who every day fill the wealthiest kitchens with the result of their labours.

This it is which supports the multitude of cooks, pastry-cooks, confectioners, etc., who employ workmen of every kind, and who perpetually put in circulation, an amount of money which the shrewdest calculator cannot imagine.

Let us observe that the trades and occupations dependent on gourmandise have this great advantage, that on one hand it is sustained by great misfortunes and on the other by accidents which happen from day to day.

In the state of society we now have reached, it is difficult to conceive of a people subsisting merely on bread and vegetables. Such a nation if it existed would certainly be subjected by carnivorous enemies, as the Hindoos were, to all who ever chose to attack them. If not it would be converted by the cooks of its neighbors as the Beotiens were, after the battle of Leuctres.

SEQUEL

Gourmandise offers great resources to fiscality, for it increases customs, imports, etc. All we consume pays tribute in one degree or another, and there is no source of public revenue to which gourmands do not contribute.

Let us speak for a moment of that crowd of preparers who every year leave France, to instruct foreign nations in gourmandise. The majority succeed and obedient to the unfasting instinct of a Frenchman's fever, return to their country with the fruits of their economy. This return is greater than one would think.

Were nations grateful, to what rather than to gourmandise should France erect a monument.

POWER OF GOURMANDISE

In 1815, the treaty of the month of November, imposed on France the necessity of paying the allies in three years, 750,000,000 francs.

Added to this was the necessity of meeting the demands of individuals of various nations, for whom the allied sovereigns had stipulated, to the amount of more than 300,000,000.

To this must be added requisitions of all kinds by the generals of the enemies who loaded whole wagons, which they sent towards the frontier, and which the treasury ultimately had to pay for. The total was more than 1,500,000,000 francs.

One might, one almost should have feared, that such large payments, collected from day to day, would have produced want in the treasury, a deprecation of all fictitious values, and consequently all the evils which befall a country that has no money, while it owes much.

"Alas," said the rich, as they saw the wagon going to the *Rue Vivienne* for its load; "all our money is emigrating, next year we will bow down to a crown: we are utterly ruined; all our undertakings will fail, and we will not be able to borrow. There will be nothing but ruin and civil death."

The result contradicted all these fears; the payments, to the amazement of financiers, were made without trouble, public credit increased, and all hurried after loans. During the period of this superpurgation, the course of exchange, an infallible measure of the circulating of money, was in our favor. This was an arithmetical proof that more money came into France than left it.

What power came to our aid? What divinity operated this miracle? Gourmandise.

When the Britons, Germans, Teutons, Cimmerians, and Scythes, made an irruption into France, they came with extreme voracity and with stomachs of uncommon capacity.

They were not long contented with the cheer furnished them by a forced hospitality, but aspired to more delicate enjoyments. The Queen City, ere long, became one immense refectory. The new comers ate in shops, cafes, restaurants, and even in the streets.

They gorged themselves with meat, fish, game, truffles, pastry and fruit.

They drank with an avidity quite equal to their appetite, and always called for the most costly wine, expecting in those unknown enjoyments, pleasures they did not meet with.

Superficial observers could not account for this eating, without hunger, which seemed limitless. All true Frenchmen, however, rubbed their hands, and said, "they are under the charm; they have spent this evening more money than they took from the treasury in the morning."

This epoch was favorable to all those who contributed to the gratification of the taste. Very made his fortune, Achard laid the foundation of his, and Madame Sullot, the shop of whom, in the Palais Royal, was not twenty feet square, sold twelve thousand *petits patés* a day.

The effect yet lasts, for strangers crowd to Paris from all parts of Europe, to rest from the fatigues of war. Our public monuments, it may be, are not so attractive as the pleasures of gourmandise, everywhere elaborated in Paris, a city essentially gourmand.

A LADY GOURMAND

Gourmandise is not unbecoming to women: it suits the delicacy of their organs and recompenses them for some pleasures they cannot enjoy, and for some evils to which they are doomed.

Nothing is more pleasant than to see a pretty woman, her napkin well placed under her arms, one of her hands on the table, while the other carries to her mouth, the choice piece so elegantly carved. Her eyes become brilliant, her lips glow, her conversation is agreeable and all her motions become graceful. With so many advantages she is irresistible, and even Cato, the censor, would feel himself moved.

ANECDOTE

I will here record what to me is a bitter reflection.

I was one day most commodiously fixed at table, by the side of the pretty Madame M−−d, and was inwardly rejoicing at having obtained such an advantageous position, when she said "your health." I immediately began a complimentary phrase, which however, I did not finish, for turning to her neighbor on the right, she said "*Trinquons*," they touched each others glasses. This quick transition seemed a perfidy, and the passage of many years have not made me forget it.

ARE WOMEN GOURMANDS?

The *penchant* of the fair sex for gourmandise is not unlike instinct; for gourmandise is favorable to beauty.

A series of exact and rigorous examinations, has shown that a succulent and delicate person on careful diet, keeps the appearance of old age long absent.

It makes the eyes more brilliant, and the color more fresh. It makes the muscles stronger, and as the depression of the muscles causes wrinkles, those terrible enemies of beauty, it is true that other things being equal, those who know how to eat, are ten years younger than those ignorant of that science.

Painters and sculptors are well aware of this, for they never represent those to whom abstinence is a matter of duty, such as anchorites and misers, except as pale, thin, and wrinkled.

THE EFFECTS OF GOURMANDISE ON SOCIABILITY

Gourmandise is one of the principle bonds of society. It gradually extends that spirit of conviviality, which every day unites different professions, mingles them together, and diminishes the angles of conviviality.

This it is, which induces every amphitryon to receive his guests well, and also excites the gratitude of the latter when they see themselves well taken care of: here is the place to reprobate those stupid masticators, who with the most guilty indifference to the greatest luxuries, and who with sacrilegious indifference inhale the odorous perfume of nectar.

GENERAL LAW.–Every display of high intelligence, makes explicit praise necessary. Delicate praise is necessary, wherever a wish to please is evident.

INFLUENCE OF GOURMANDISE ON CONJUGAL HAPPINESS

When gourmandise is shared with another, it has the greatest influence on conjugal happiness.

A gourmand couple have at least once a day a pleasant occasion to meet, for even those who sleep apart (and there are many) dine together. They talk of what they have eaten, of what they have seen elsewhere, of fashionable dishes and of new inventions, etc., etc. We all know how full of charms this CHIT CHAT is.

Music, doubtless, has many charms for those who love it; but to succeed, one must make a business of it.

Besides, sometimes one has a cold, misplaces the score, has the sick headache or feels inert.

One necessity calls each of the couple to the table, where the same feeling retains them. They exhibit naturally slight attentions to each other, which evinces a desire to please, and the manner in which they act to each other speaks loudly of the manner of their lives.

This observation, though new in France, has not escaped the attention of the English novelist, Fielding, who in Pamela gives the well-known instance of the manner in which the heroine and her husband lived on the one hand, and the more magnificent but unhappy life of the elder brother and his wife.

Honour then to gourmandise as we present it to our readers, inasmuch as it diverts man neither from occupation nor from duty; for as the dissoluteness of Sardanapulus did not cause the world to look on woman with horror, neither did Vitellius' excesses induce the world to turn aside from a well-ordered entertainment.

When gourmandise becomes gluttony, voracity or debauchery, it loses its name and attributes, falling into the hands of the moralist who will treat it by advice, or the medical man who will treat it by remedy.

Gourmandise, as the professor has described it, has a name only in French; neither the Latin gula, English "*gluttony*" nor German *lusternheit*, expresses it, and we recommend all who attempt a translation of this instructive book to preserve the word, changing the article which produces it only. Thus they did with *coquetterie*.

NOTE OF A PATRIOT GASTRONOMER

"I observe with pride, that gourmandise and coquettery, the two great modifications which society has effected in our imperious wants, are both of French origin."

MEDITATION XII

GOURMANDS

ALL WHO WISH TO BE ARE NOT GOURMANDS

THERE are individuals to whom nature has refused a fineness of organs and a degree of attention, without which the most succulent food passes unperceived.

Physiology has already recognized the first of these varieties, by exhibiting the tongue of those unfortunate men who are badly provided with the means of appreciating flavors and tastes. Such persons have but an obtuse sensation, for to them taste is what light is to the blind.

The second of these varieties is composed of absent minded men, of ambitious persons, and others, who wish to attend to two things at once, and who eat only to eat.

NAPOLEON

Such was Napoleon; he was irregular in his meals and ate quickly. When hungry, his appetite had to be satisfied at once, and he was so completely *served*, that at any hour he could have fowl, game or coffee.

GOURMANDS BY DESTINY

There is however, a privileged class, which organic and material organization invites to the enjoyments of the taste.

I was always a disciple of Lavater and Gall, and believe in innate ideas.

As persons have been born who see, walk, and hear badly, because they are near-sighted, lame, or deaf, why may there not be others inclined to peculiar sensations.

To the most careless observer there will ever be presented faces which bear the undeniable expression of some dominant sentiment, such as disdainful impertinence, self-satisfaction, misanthropy, sensuality, &c. A very meaningless face may express all this, but when the face has a determined expression, one is rarely mistaken.

Passions agitate the muscles, and often when a man is silent, the various feelings which agitate him may be read on his face. This tension, though habitual leave sensible traces, and give the face a permanent and well defined character.

SENSUAL PREDESTINATION

The persons predestined to gourmandise are in general of medium stature. Their faces are either round or square, and small, their noses short and their chins rounded. The women are rather pretty than beautiful, and they have a slight tendency to obesity.

Those who are fondest of *friandises* have delicate features, smaller, and are distinguished by a peculiar expression of the mouth.

Agreeable guests should be sought for among those who have this appearance. They receive all that is offered them, eat slowly, and taste advisedly. They do not seek to leave places too quickly where they have been kindly received. They are always in for all the evening, for they know all games, and all that is neccessary for a gastronomical *soirée*.

Those, on the contrary, to whom nature has refused a desire for the gratifications of taste, have a long nose and face. Whatever be their statures, the face seems out of order. Their hair is dark and flat, and they have no *embonpoint*. They invented pantaloons.

Women whom nature has thus afflicted, are very angulous, are uncomfortable at the table, and live on lenten fare.

This physiological theory will, I trust, meet with not many contradictions: any one may verify the matter. I will, however, rely on facts.

I was sitting one day at a great entertainment, and saw opposite to me a very pretty woman with a very sensual face. I leaned towards my neighbor and said, that the lady with such features must be *gourmande*. "Bah!" said he, "she is not more than fifteen; she is not old enough—let us see though."

The beginning was not favorable, and I was afraid of being compromised. During the first two courses, the young woman ate with a discretion which really amazed me. The dessert came, it was brilliant as it was abundant, and gave me some hopes. I was not deceived, for she not only ate what was set before her, but sent for dishes which were at the other end of the table. She tasted every thing, and we were surprised that so small a stomach could contain so much. My diagnostics succeeded and science triumphed.

Two years after I met this same lady, who had been married a week. She had become far more beautiful, was something of a *coquette*, for fashion permitted her to exhibit her charms. Her husband was a man worth looking at, but he was like one of those ventriloquists who laugh on one side of the face and weep on the other. He was very fond of his wife, but when any one spoke to her, quivered with jealousy. The latter sentiment prevailed, for he took his wife to one of the most remote departments of France, and I, *at least*, can write no more of her biography.

I made a similar observation about the Duke of Decrès, long minister of marine.

We knew that he was large, short, dark and square; that his face was round, that his chin protruded, that his lips were thick, and that he had a giant's mouth. I therefore had no hesitation in proclaiming him fond of good cheer and of women.

This physiognomical remark I whispered to a woman I thought very pretty and very discreet. I was mistaken though, for she was a daughter of Eve, and my secret was made known. One evening his excellency was informed of the idea I had deduced from his face.

I ascertained this the next day, by a pleasant letter which I received from the Duke, in which he insisted that he had not the two qualities I had attributed to him.

I confessed myself beaten. I replied that nature does nothing in vain; that she had evidently formed him for certain duties, and that if he did not fulfil them he contradicted his appearance. That besides, I had no right to expect such confidence, etc., etc.

There the correspondence terminated, but a few days after all Paris was amused by the famous encounter between the minister and his cook, in which his excellency did not get the best of the matter. If after such an affair the cook was not dismissed, (and he was not,) I may conclude that the duke was completely overcome by the artist's talents, and that he could not find another one to suit his taste so exactly, otherwise he would have gotten rid of so warlike a servant.

As I wrote these lines, during a fine winter evening, Mr. Cartier, once first violinist of the opera, entered my room and sat by the fire. I was full of my subject, and looked attentively at him. I said, "My dear Professor, how comes it that you, who have every feature of gourmandise, are not a gourmand?" "I am," said he, "but I make abstinence a duty." "Is that an act of prudence?" He did not reply, but he uttered a sigh, *a la* Walter Scott.

GOURMANDS BY PROFESSION

If there be gourmands by predestination, there are also gourmands by profession. There are four classes of these: Financiers, men of letters, doctors, and devotees.

FINANCIERS

Financiers are the heroes of gourmandise. Hero is here the proper name, for there was some contention, and the men who had titles crowd all others beneath their titles and escutcheons. They would have triumphed, but for the wealth of those they opposed. Cooks contended with genealogists; and though dukes did not fail to laugh at their amphitryon, they came to the dinner, and that was enough.

Those persons who make money easily must be *gourmands*.

The inequality of wealth produces inequality of wants. He who can pay every day for a dinner fit for an hundred persons, is often satisfied after having eaten the thigh of a chicken. Art then must use well its resources to revive appetite. Thus Mondar became a gourmand, and others with the same tastes collects around him.

PHYSICIANS

Causes of another nature, though far less baneful, act on physicians, who, from the nature of things, are gourmands. To resist the attractions set before them they must necessarily be made of bronze.

One day I ventured to say, (Doctor Corvisart was at the end of the table–the time was about 1806):–

"You are," said I, with the air of an inspired puritan, "the last remnant of a composition which once covered all France. The members of it are either annihilated or dispersed. No longer do we see farmers general, abbes, chevaliers, &c. Bear the burden they have bequeathed to you, even if you take the three hundred Spartans who died at Thermopylae; such a fate should be yours."

Nobody contradicted me.

At dinner I made a remark which was worthy of notice:–

Doctor Corvisart was a very pleasant man when he pleased, and was very fond of iced champagne. For this reason, while all the rest of the company were dull and idle, he dealt in anecdotes and stories. On the contrary, when the dessert was put on, and conversation became animated, he became serious and almost morose.

From this and other observations, I deduced the following conclusion: Champagne, the first effect of which is exhilarating, in the result is stupefying, on account of the excessant carbonic gases it contains.

OBJUGATION

As I measure doctors by their *diplomatu*, I will not reproach them for the severity with which they treat their invalids.

As soon as one has the misfortune to fall into their hands, one has to give up all we have previously thought agreeable.

I look on the majority of these prohibitions as useless. I say useless, because patients never desire what is injurious to them.

A reasonable physician should never lose sight of the natural tendency of our inclinations, nor forget to ascertain if our *penchants* are painful in themselves, or improving to health. A little wine, or a few drops of liquor, brings the smiles to the most hypochondriac faces.

Besides, they know that their severe prescriptions are almost always without effect, and the patient seeks to avoid him. Those who are around him, never are in want of a reason to gratify him. People, however, will die.

The ration of a sick Russian, in 1815, would have made a porter drunk. There was no retrenchment to be made, for military inspectors ran from day to day through the hospitals, and watched over the furnishment and the service of the various houses.

I express my opinions with the more confidence, because it is sustained by much experience, and that the most fortunate practitioners rely on my system.

The canon Rollet who died about fifty years ago, was a great drinker; and the first physician he employed, forbid him to use wine at all. When, however, he came again, the doctor found his patient in bed, and before him the *corpus delicti*, i.e., a table covered with a white cloth, a chrystal cup, a handsome bottle, and a napkin to wipe his lips with.

The doctor at once became enraged, and was about to withdraw, when the canon said in a lamentable voice, "doctor, remember, if you forbade my drinking, you did not prohibit my looking at the bottle."

The physician who attended M. Montlusin de Point de Veyle was far more cruel, for he not only forbid his patient to touch wine, but made him drink large quantities of water.

A short time after the doctor had left, Mme. de Montlusin, anxious to fulfil the requisition of the prescription, and contribute to her husband's recovery, gave him a great glass of water, pure and limpid as possible.

The patient received it kindly and sought to drink it with resignation. At the first swallow, however, he stopped, and giving the glass back to his wife, said, "Take this, dear, and keep it for the next dose; I have always heard, one should never trifle with remedies."

MEN OF LETTERS

Men of letters in the world of gastronomy, have a place nearly equal to that of men of medical faculty.

Under the reign of Louis XIV., men of letters were all given to drink. They conformed to fashion and the memoirs of the day, in this respect, are very defying. They are now *gourmands*,–a great amelioration.

I am far from agreeing with the cynic Geoffroy, who used to say that modern works were deficient in power because authors now drank only *eau sucrée*.

I think he made two mistakes, both in the fact and the consequences.

The age we live in is rich in talents; they injure each other perhaps by their multitude; but posterity, judging with more calmness, will see much to admire. Thus we do justice to the great productions of Racine and Molière which when written were coldly received.

The social position of men of letters was never more agreeable. They no longer live in the garrets they used to inhabit, for the field of literature has become fertile. The stream of Hippocrène rolls down golden sands: equals of all, they never hear the language of protection, and gourmandise overwhelms them with its choicest favours.

Men of letters are courted on account of their talent, and because their conversation is in general *piquant*, and because it has for some time been established, that every society should have its man of letters.

These gentlemen always come a little too late: they are not however received the most on that account, for they have been anxiously expected: they are petted up to induce them to come again, are flattered to make them brilliant, and as they find all this very natural, they grow used to it and become genuine gourmands.

DEVOTEES

Among the friends of gourmandise are many very devout persons.

By the word devotee, we understand what Louis XIV. and Molière did, persons the piety of whom consists in external observances; pious and charitable persons have nothing to do with this class.

Let us see how they effect this—among those who work out their salvation, the greatest number seek the mildest method. Those who avoid society, sleep on the ground and wear hair cloth, are always exceptions.

Now there are to them certain damnable things never to be permitted, such as balls, plays, and other amusements.

While they and those who enjoy them are abominated, gourmandise assumes an altogether different aspect, and becomes almost theological.

Jure divinô, man is the king of nature and all that earth creates was produced for him. For him the quail becomes fat, the mocha has its perfume, and sugar becomes beneficial to the health.

Why then should we not use with suitable moderation the goods which Providence offers us, especially as we continue to look on them as perishable things, and as they exalt our appreciation of the Creator.

Other not less weighty reasons strengthen these—can we receive too kindly those persons who take charge of our souls? Should we not make a meeting with them pleasant and agreeable?

Sometimes the gifts of Comus come unexpectedly. An old college companion, an old friend, a penitent who humbles himself, a kinsman who makes himself known or a protégé recalls them.

This has ever been the case.

Convents were the true warehouses of the most adorable delacies: for that reason they have been so much regretted.[30]

Many monastic orders, especially the Bernardins paid great attention to good cheer. The cooks of the clergy reached the very limits of the art, and M. de Pressigny (who died Archbishop of Besançon) returned from the conclave which elected *Pio Sesto*, he said the best dinner he ate in Rome was given by the General of the Capuchins.

CHEVALIERS AND ABBÉS

We cannot bring this article to a better end than to make an honourable mention of two corporations we saw in all their glory: we mean the Chevaliers and the Abbes.

How completely gourmand they were. Their expanded nostrils, their acute eyes, and coral lips could not he mistaken, neither could their gossiping tongue; each class, however, ate in a peculiar manner.

There was something military in the bearing of the Chevaliers. They ate their delicacies with dignity, worked calmly, and cast horizontal looks of approbation at both the master and mistress of the house.

The Abbes however, used to come to the table with more care, and reached out their hands as the cat snatches chestnuts from the fire. Their faces were all enjoyment, and there was a concentration about their looks more easy to conceive of, than to describe.

As three-fourths of the present generation have seen nothing like either the Abbes, or Chevaliers, and as it is necessary to understand them, to be able to appreciate many books written in the eighteenth century, we will borrow from the author of the Historical Treatise on Duels, a few pages which will fully satisfy all persons about this subject. (*See Varieties, No. 20.*)

---

[30] The best liquors in France were made of the Visitandines. The monks of Niort invented the conserve of Angelica, and the bread flavoured with orange flowers by the notes of Château-Thierry is yet famous. The nuns of Belley used also to make a delicious conserve of nuts. Alas, it is lost, I am afraid.

LONGEVITY OF GOURMANDS.

I am happy, I cannot be more so, to inform my readers that good cheer is far from being injurious, and that all things being equal, gourmands live longer than other people. This was proved by a scientific dissertation recently read at the academy, by Doctor Villermet.

He compares the different states of society, in which good cheer is attended to, with those where no attention is paid to it, and has passed through every scale of the ladder. He has compared the various portions of Paris, in which people were more or less comfortable. All know that in this respect there is extreme difference, as for instance between the Faubourg St. Antoine and the Chaussée d' Antin.

The doctor extended his research to the departments of France, and compared the most sterile and fertile together, and always obtained a general result in favor of the diminution of mortality, in proportion universally as the means of subsistence improve. Those who cannot well sustain themselves will be at least wise, to know that death will deliver them soon.

The two extremes of this progression are, that in the most highly favored ranks of life but one individual in fifty dies, while of those who are poorer four do.

Those who indulge in good cheer, are rarely, or never sick. Alas! they often fall into the domain of the faculty, who call them *good patients*: as however they have no great degree of vitality, and all portions of their organization are better sustained, nature has more resources, and the body incomparably resists destruction.

This physiological truth may be also sustained by history, which tells us that as often as impervious circumstances, such as war, sieges, the derangement of seasons, etc., diminish the means of subsistence, such times have ever been accompanied by contagious disease and a great increase of mortality.

The idea of Lafarge would beyond a doubt have succeeded in Paris, if those who had advanced it had introduced into their calculations the truths developed by Doctor Villermet.

They calculated mortality according to Buffoon's tables, and those of Parcieux and others, all of which were based on the aggregate of all classes and conditions. Those who made the estimate, however, forgot the dangers of infancy, indulged in general calculations, and the speculation failed.

This may not have been the only, hut it was the principal cause.

For this observation, we are indebted to the Professor Pardessus.

M. de Belloy, archbishop of Paris, had a slight appetite, but a very distinct one. He loved good cheer and I have often seen his patriarchal face lighten up at the appearance of any choice dish. Napoleon always on such occasions paid him deference and respect.

MEDITATION XIII

GASTRONOMICAL TESTS

IN the preceding chapter, we have seen that the distinctive characteristics of those who have more pretension than right to the honors of gourmandise, consists in the fact, that, at the best spread table, their eyes are dull and their face inanimate.

They are not worthy of having treasures, when they do not appreciate what is exhibited to them. It, however, was very interesting for us to point them out, and we have sought every where for information on so important a matter, as who should be our guests and our hosts.

We set about this with an anxiety which ensures success, and, in consequence of our perseverance, we are able to present to the corps of amphitryon, gastronomical tests, a discovery which will do honor to the nineteenth century.

By gastronomical tests, we mean dishes of so delicious a flavor that their very appearance excites the gustatory organs of every healthy man. The consequence is, that all those who do not evince desire, and the radiancy of ecstasy, may very properly be set down as unworthy of the honours of the society and the pleasures attached to them.

The method of TESTS duly deliberated on, and examined in the great council, has been described in the golden book, in words of an unchangeable tongue, as follows:

Utcumque ferculum, eximii et bene noti saporis appositum fuerit, fiat autopsia convivoe; et nisi facies ejus ae oculi vertantur ad ecstasim, notetur ut indignus.

This was rendered into the vernacular, by the translator of the grand council, as follows:

"Whenever a dish of a distinguished and good flavor is served, the guests should be attentively watched, and those, the faces of whom do not express pleasure, should be marked as unworthy."

Tests are relative, and should be proportioned to the various classes of society. All things considered, it should be arranged so as to create admiration and surprise. It is a dynameter, the power of which should increase as we ascend in society. The test for a householder in *La Rue Coquenard*, would not suit a second clerk, and would be unnoticed at the table of a financier, or a minister.

In the enumeration of the dishes we think worthy of being considered as tests, we will begin at the lowest grade, and will gradually ascend so as to elucidate the theory, so that all may not only use it with benefit, but also invent a new series calculated for the sphere in which they chance to be placed.

We will now give a list of the dishes we think fit to be served as tests; we have divided them into three series of gradual ascents, following the order indicated above.

GASTRONOMICAL TESTS

FIRST SERIES. –INCOME OF 5,000 FRANCS

A breast of veal baked in its own juice.
A turkey stuffed with Lyons chestnuts.
Baked pigeons.
Eggs *a la neige*.
Sourkrout, with sausages dressed with lard, *fume de Strasburg*.
EXPRESSION. "Peste; that looks well; let us pay our devoirs to it."

SECOND SERIES.–INCOME 15,000 FRANCS

A *filet de boeuf piqué*, and baked in its juice, with pickles.
A quarter of *Chevreuil*.
Turbot plain.
A Turkey Truffee.
Petits pois.
EXCLAMATION. "My dear sir, this is pleasant indeed!"

THIRD SERIES. –INCOME 30,000 FRANCS, OR MORE

A fowl weighing seven pounds, stuffed with truffles, so that it has become a spheroid.
A *patté perigord* in the form of a bastion.

A cask *a la Chambord* richly dressed and decorated.

A pike stuffed with crawfish *secundum artum*.

A pheasant dressed *a la sainte alliance*.

Asparagus, large as possible, served up in osmazome.

Two dozen ortolans *a la provencale*, as the dish is described in the Cook's Secretary.

A pyramid of sweet meats, flavored with rose and vanilla.

EXPRESSION. "Monsieur, or Monseigneur, your cook is a man of mind. Such dishes we eat only at your house."

MEDITATION XIV

ON THE PLEASURES OF THE TABLE

MAN of all the animals who live on the earth, is beyond doubt, the one who experiences most suffering.

Nature condemned him to suffering by robbing him of hair, by giving him such a peculiar formation of his feet, also by the instinct of destruction, and of war which has followed man every where.

Animals have never been stricken with this curse, and with the exception of a few contests, caused by the instinct of reproduction, harm would be absolutely unknown to the lower animals of creation. Man, though he cannot appreciate pleasure except by a small number of organs, may yet be liable to intense agony.

This decree of destiny was engraved by a crowd of maladies, which originated in the social system. The result is that the most intense pleasure one can imagine, cannot atone for certain pains, such as the gout, the tooth-ache, etc., acute rheumatisms, strictures, and many other diseases we might mention.

This practical fear of pain has had the effect, that without even perceiving it, man has rushed into an opposite direction, and has devoted himself to the small number of pleasures nature has placed at his disposal.

ORIGIN OF THE PLEASURES OF THE TABLE

Meals, as we understand the word, began at the second stage of the history of humanity. That is to say as soon as we ceased to live on fruits alone. The preparation and distribution of food made the union of the family a necessity, at least once a day. The heads of families then distributed the produce of the chase, and grown children did as much for their parents.

These collections, limited at first to near relations, were ultimately extended to neighbors and friends.

At a later day when the human species was more widely extended, the weary traveler used to sit at such boards and tell what he had seen in foreign lands. Thus hospitality was produced, and its rights were recognized everywhere. There was never any one so ferocious as not to respect him who had partaken of his bread and salt.

DIFFERENCE BETWEEN THE PLEASURE OF EATING AND THE PLEASURES OF THE TABLE

Such from the nature of things, should be the elements of the pleasures of the table which, where eating is a necessity, of course takes the precedence.

The pleasure of eating is a peculiar sensation directed to the satisfaction of a necessity. The pleasures of the table is a reflected sensation, originating in various facts, places, things and persons.

We share with animals in the pleasure of eating. They and we have hunger which must he satisfied.

It is peculiar to the human race, for it supposes a predisposition for food, for the place of meeting, and for guests.

The pleasures of the table exact, if not hunger, at least appetite. The table is often independent of both the one and the other.

This we may see at every entertainment.

At the first course every one eats and pays no attention to conversation; all ranks and grades are forgotten together in the great manufacture of life. When, however, hunger begins to be satisfied, reflection begins, and conversation commences. The person who, hitherto, had been a mere consumer, becomes an amiable guest, in proportion as the master of all things provides him with the means of gratification.

EFFECTS

The pleasures of the table afford neither ravishing pleasure, ecstasy, nor transport, but it gains in intensity what it loses in duration. It is the more valuable because it exposes us to all other gratifications and even consoles us for their loss.

After a good dinner body and soul enjoy a peculiar happiness.

Physically, as the brain becomes refreshed, the face lightens up, the colors become heightened, and a glow spreads over the whole system.

Morally, the mind becomes sharpened, witticisms circulate. If La Farre and Saint Aulaire descend to posterity with the reputation of spiritual authors, they owe it especially to the fact that they were pleasant guests.

Besides, there are often found collected around the same table, all the modifications of society which extreme sociability has introduced among us: love, friendship, business, speculation, power, ambition, and intrigue, all enhance conviviality. Thus it is that it produces fruits of all imaginable flavors.

ACCESSORIES

An immediate consequence of all these antecedents is that human industry has toiled to augment the duration of the gratifications of the table.

Poets complain that the throat is too short for the uses of degustation, and others lament the want of capacity of the stomach. Some even regret that digestion is accomplished in a single act and not divided into two.

This was but an extreme effort to amplify the enjoyments of taste; in this respect, however, it is impossible to exceed the limits imposed by nature, and an appeal was made to accessories, which offered more latitude.

Vases and goblets were crowned with flowers; crowns were distributed to the guests, and dinners served beneath the vault of heaven, in groves, and amid all the wonders of nature.

Music and song were made to increase the pleasures of the table. Thus while the king of the Pheacians ate, the singer Phemius sang the praises of the wars and warriors of other days.

Often dancers and pantomimists of both sexes, in all possible costumes, occupied the attention without injuring the pleasure of the meal. The most exquisite perfumes were diffused in the air, and guests were often waited on by unveiled beauty, so that every sense was appealed to.

I might consume many pages in proving what I advance. The Greek authors and our old chroniclers only need to be copied. These researches, however, only need to be made to be evident, and my erudition would be of little value

THE 18TH AND 19TH CENTURY

We have adopted to a greater or less degree various methods of enjoyment, and have, by new discoveries, somewhat enhanced the number.

The delicacy of our tastes would not permit the vomitoria of the Romans to remain. We did better, however, and accomplished the same object in a more pleasant manner.

Dishes of such an attractive flavor have been increased that they perpetually reproduce the appetite. They are so light that they flatter the appetite without loading the stomach. Seneca would have called them NUBES ESCULENTAS.

We have advanced so far in alimentation that if business called us from the table, or if it became necessary for us to sleep, the duration of the meal would have been almost indeterminable.

One must not, however, believe that all of these accessories are indispensable to the pleasures of the table. Pleasure is enjoyed in almost all its extent when the following conditions are united: good cheer, good wine, a pleasant company, and time.

I have often, therefore, wished to have been present at one of those pleasant repasts which Horace invited one of his neighbors to share, viz: a good chicken, a lamb (doubtless fat,) and as a desert, grapes, figs and nuts. Uniting these to wine, made when Manlius was consul, and the delicious conversation of the poet, I fancy I could have supped very pleasantly.

At mihi cum longum post tempus venerat hospes
Sive operum vacuo, longum conviva per imbrem
Vicinus, bene erat non piscibus urbe petitis,
Sed pullo atque hasdo, tum[31] pensilis uva secundas
Et nux ornabat mensas, cum duplice ficu.

Thus it was only yesterday I regaled six friends with a boiled leg of mutton and a kidney A L'PONTOISE. They indulged in the pleasures of conversation so fully that they forgot that there were richer meats or better cooks.

---

[31] Footnote: Le dessert se trouve precisement designe et distingue par l'adverbe TUM et par les mots SECUNDAS MENSAS.

On the other hand, let persons make as much research as possible for good cheer; there is no pleasure at the table if the wine be bad, and the guests collected without care. Faces will then be sure to seem sad, and the meal will be eaten without, consideration.

SUMMARY

But perhaps the impatient reader will ask how, in the year of grace 1825, can any table be spread which will unite all of these conditions?

I will answer this question. Be attentive, readers. Gasterea, the most attractive of the muses, inspires me. I will be as clear as an oracle, and my precepts will live for centuries:–

"Let the number of guests never exceed twelve, so that the conversation may be general.

"Let them he so chosen that their occupations may be varied, their tastes analogous, and that they may have such points of contact that introduction may be useless.

"Let the dining-room be furnished with luxury, the table clean, and the temperature of the room about 16 degrees Réaumur.

"Let the men be intelligent, but not pedantic–and the women pretty, but not coquettes.

"Let the dishes be of exquisite taste, but few in number at the first course; let those of the second be as pleasant and as highly perfumed as possible.

"Let the coffee be hot, and let the master select his own wines.

"Let the reception-room be large enough to permit those who cannot do without the amusement, to make up a card party, and also for little COTERIES of conversation.

"Let the guests be retained by the pleasures of society, and by the hope that the evening will not pass without some ulterior enjoyment

"The tea should not be too strong, the roast dishes should be loaded artistically, and the punch made carefully.

"None should begin to retire before eleven o'clock, and at midnight all should have gone to bed.

"If any one has been present at an entertainment uniting all these conditions, he may boast of having witnessed his own apotheosis. He will enjoy it the more, because many other apotheosis have been forgotten or mistaken."

I have said that the pleasure of the table, as I have described it, was susceptible of long duration, and I am about to prove it by the history of the longest meal I ever was present at. It is a BONBON I give the reader as a reward for patient attention to me. Here it is:-

I had a family of kinsfolk in the Rue de Bac, constituted as follows: a doctor, who was seventy-eight; a captain, who was seventy-six; and their sister, Jeannette, who was sixty-four. I used to visit them sometimes, and they always received me kindly.

"PARBLEU!" said Doctor Dubois, rising on his toes one day to tap me on the shoulder; "you have a long time been bragging about your FONDUES, (eggs and cheese,) and you always make our mouths water. The captain and I will come to dine with you, and we will see what your famous dish is." (This took place about 1801.) "Willingly," said I, "and to enable you to see it in all its glory, I will cook it myself. I am delighted with your proposition, and wish you to come punctually at ten to-morrow."

At the appointed time my guests came, clean shaved, and with their heads powdered. They were two little old men; yet fresh, however, and well.

They smiled with pleasure when they saw the table ready, set with three covers, and with two dozen oysters by each plate.

At the two ends of the table were bottles of Sauterne, carefully wiped, except the cork, which indicated that it had been long bottled.

Alas! I have gradually seen oysters disappear from breakfast, though they were once so common. They disappeared with the ABBES, who never ate less than a gross; and the CHEVALIERS, who ate quite as many. I regret them but as a philosopher. If time modifies governments, how great must be its influence over simple usages.

After the oysters, which were very good, grilled kidneys, a PATE of FOIE GRAS with truffles, and then the FONDUE.

The elements had been put in a chafing-dish, and brought to the table with spirits of wine. I set at once to work, and my two cousins watched every motion I made.

They were delighted, and asked for the recipe, which I promised, telling them two anecdotes, which the reader will perhaps meet with elsewhere.

After the FONDUE we had the various fruits which were in season, and a cup of real mocha, made A LA DU BELLOY, which was then becoming fashionable. We ended with two kinds of LIQUEURS.

Breakfast being over, I invited my two kinsmen to take a little exercise, and to accompany me through my lodgings, which are far from being elegant, and which my friends, in consequence of their size and splendor, prefer to the gilding and OR MOLU of the reign of Louis XV.

I showed them the original bust of my pretty cousin, Mme. Recamier by Chinard, and her miniature by Augustin. They were so much pleased, that the Doctor kissed the latter with his thick lips, and the Captain took a liberty with the bust of the first, for which I reproved him. Were all the admirers of the original to do as he did, the bust would soon be in the condition of the famous statue of St. Peter at Borne, which the kisses of pilgrims have worn away.

I showed them afterwards, casts of old statuary, some pictures, which are not without merit, my guns, my musical instruments, and several fine editions of the French and foreign classics.

They did not forget the kitchen in their voyage of discovery. I showed them my economical furnace, my turnspit by clockwork, my roasting apparatus, and my vaporiser. They were much surprised, as every thing in their house was done in the style of the regency.

Just as we were about to enter the room, the clock struck two. "Peste!" said the Doctor, "the dinner time and Jeannette awaits us; we must go, not because I wish to eat, but I must have my bowl of soup like Titus DIEM PERDIDI." "My dear Doctor," said I, "why go so far? what is here? Send some to my cousin and remain here, if you will, and accept my apology for a somewhat hasty dinner and you will delight me."

There was an ocular consultation on the matter between the two brothers, and I at once sent a messenger to the Faubourg St. Germain. I also told my cook what I wished. After a time, in part with his own resources and from the neighboring restaurants, he served us up a very comfortable little dinner.

It was a great gratification to me, to see the SANG FROID and quiet nerve with which my kinsmen sat down, unfolded their napkins and began. They met with two surprises which I did not anticipate; I gave them PARMESAN with soup, and a glass of dry Madeira. These two novelties had just been introduced by M. De Tallyrand, the first of our diplomatists, to whom we are indebted for so many shrewd expressive words, and whom public attention has always followed with marked interest even when he had retired.

Dinner passed very comfortably, and as far as the substantiate and the accessories were concerned, my friends were as agreeable as they were merry.

After dinner, I proposed a game of PIQUET, which they refused, preferring, as the Captain said, IL FAR NIENTE of the Italians, and we sat around the fireplace.

In spite of the pleasures of the FAR NIENTE, I have often thought that nothing enlivens conversation more than any occupation which distracts but does not absorb all conversation.

Tea was a novelty to the French at that time. They however took it; I made it in their presence, and they took it with greater pleasure, because, hitherto they had only looked on it as a remedy.

Long observation had informed me, that one piece of complaisance ever brings on another, and that after one step there is no choice but to continue in the same route.

"You will kill me," said the Doctor. "You will make me drunk," said the Captain. I made no reply, but rang for rum, sugar, and lemons. I made some punch, and while I was preparing some, excellent well buttered toast was also prepared.

My cousins protested that they could not eat a morsel more; but, as I was familiar with the attraction of this simple preparation, I insisted, and the Captain having taken the first slice, I had no hesitation in ordering more.

Time rolled on, and the clock was on the stroke of eight. "Let us go," said the worthies, "for we must eat a salad with our sister, who has not seen us to day."

I did not object, and accompanied the two pleasant old men to their carriage, and saw them leave.

Perhaps, the question may be asked, if their long visit did not annoy me.

I answer, no. The attention of my guests was sustained by the preparation of the FONDUE, by their examination of my rooms, by a few novelties after dinner, by the tea, and especially by the punch, which was the best they had ever tasted.

The Doctor, too, knew all the genealogy and history of the people of Paris. The Captain had passed a portion of his life in Italy, either as a soldier or as envoy to the Court of Parma. I had travelled much, and conversation pursued its natural bent. Under such circumstances time could not but fly rapidly.

On the next day, a letter from the Doctor informed me, that their little debauch had done them no harm, but that after a quiet night's rest, they awoke convinced that they could go over the whole matter again.

MEDITATION XV

HALTES DE CHASSE

AMID all the circumstances in life, when eating is considered valuable, one of the most agreeable is, doubtless, when there is a pause in the chase. It alone may be prolonged the most without *ennui*.

After a few hours exercise, the most eager huntsman feels a necessity for rest. His face needs caressing by the morning breeze: he halts, however, not from necessity, but by that instinctive impulse which tells him that his activity is not indefinite.

Shade attracts him, the turf receives him, the murmur of the rivulet advises him to open the flask he has brought to revive himself I with.[32] Thus placed, he takes out the little well baked loaves, uncovers the cold chicken some kind hand has placed in his havresack, and finds the piece of *Gruyere* or *Roquefort*, which is to represent a dessert.

While he makes these preparations, he is accompanied by the faithful animal God has created for him; co-operation has overcome distance. They are two friends, and the servant is at once happy and proud to be the guest of his master.

It is an appetite equally unknown to the worldly and devotees: the first do not allow hunger time to come: the second never indulge in exercises which produce it.

The repast being prepared, each has its portion; why not sleep for a while? Noon is an hour of rest for all creation.

The pleasures are *décuplés* by being shared with friends. In this case, a more abundant meal is brought in military chests now employed for both purposes. All speak of the prowess of one, the messes at the other, and of the anticipations of the evening.

What if one should come provided with one of those vases consecrated to Bacchus, where artificial cold ices the madrin, the strawberry, and pine-apple juice, those delicious flavors which spread through the whole system a luxury unknown to the profane.

We have not, however, reached the last term of progression of pleasure.

---

[32] For such purposes, I prefer white wine; it resists heat better than any other.

LADIES

There are times when our wives, sisters, and cousins are invited to share in these amusements. At the appointed hour, light carriages, prancing horses, etc., hearing ladies collect. The toilette of the ladies is half military, and half coquette. The professor will, if he be observant, catch a glimpse of things not intended for his eye.

The door of the carriages will soon be opened, and a glimpse will be had of *patés de Perigord*, the wonders of Strasburg, the delicacies of *d'Achard*, and all that the best laboratories produce that is transportable.

They have not forgotten foaming champagne, a fit ornament for the hand of beauty. They sit on the grass—corks fly, all laugh, jest, and are happy. Appetite, this emenation of heaven, gives to the meal a vivacity foreign to the drawing-room, however well decorated it may be.

All, however, must end; the oldest person present gives the signal; all arise, men take their guns, and the ladies their hats- -all go, and the ladies disappear until night.

I have hunted in the centre of France, and in the very depths of the departments. I have seen at the resting places carriage loads of women of radiant beauty, and others mounted on a modest ass, such as composes the fortunes of the people of Montmorency. I have seen them first laugh at the inconveniences of the mode of transportation, and then spread on the lawn a turkey, with transparent jelly, and a salad ready prepared. I have seen them dance around a fire lighted for the occasion, and have participated in the pleasures of this gypsy sport. I am sure so much attraction with so little luxury is never met with elsewhere.

Les haltes de la chasse are a yet virgin subject which we have only touched, we leave the subject to any one who pleases to take a fancy to it.

MEDITATION XVI

ON DIGESTION

We never see what we eat, says an old adage, except what we digest.

How few, however, know what digestion is, though it is a necessity equalizing rich and poor, the shepherd and the king.

The majority of persons who, like M. Jourdan, talked prose without knowing it, digest without knowing how; for them I make a popular history of digestion, being satisfied that M. Jourdan was much better satisfied when his master told him that he wrote prose. To he fully acquainted with digestion, one must know hoth its antecedents and consequents.

INGESTION

Appetite, hunger, and thirst, warn us that the hody needs restoration; pain, that universal monitor, never ceases to torment us if we do not obey it.

Then comes eating and drinking which are ingestion, an operation which begins as soon as the food is in the mouth, and enters the esophagus.

During its passage, through a space of a few inches much takes place.

The teeth divide solid food, the glands which line the inside of the mouth moisten it, the tongue mingles the food, presses it against the palate so as to force out the juice, and then collects the elements in the centre of the mouth, after which, resting on the lower jaw, it lifts up the central portion forming a kind of inclined plane to the lower portion of the mouth where they are received by the pharynx, which itself contracting, forces them into the esophagus.

One mouthful having thus been treated, a second is managed in the same way, and deglutition continues until appetite informs us that it is time to stop. It is rarely, though, that it stops here, for as it is one of the attributes of man to drink without thirst, cooks have taught him to eat without hunger.

To ensure every particle of food reaching the stomach, two dangers must be avoided.

It must not pass into the passage behind the nose, which luckily is covered by a veil.

The second is that it must not enter the trachea. This is a serious danger, for any particle passing into the trachea, would cause a convulsive cough, which would last until it was expelled.

An admirable mechanism, however, closes the glottis while we swallow, and we have a certain instinct which teaches us not to breathe during deglutition. In general, therefore, we may say, that in spite of this strange conformation, food passes easily into the stomach, where the exercise of the will ceases, and digestion begins.

DUTY OF THE STOMACH

Digestion is a purely mechanical operation and the digestive apparatus, may be considered as a winnowing mill, the effect of which is, to extract all that is nutritious and to get rid of the chaff.

The manner in which digestion is effcted has been so long a question for argument, and persons have sought to ascertain if it were effected by coction, fermentation, solution, chemical, or vital action.

All of these modes have their influence, and the only error was that many causes were sought to be attributed to one.

In fact food impregnated by all fluids which fill the mouth and oesophagus, reaches the stomach where it is impregnated by the gastric juices, which always fill it. It is then subjected for several hours to a heat of 30 [degrees] Reaumer; it is mingled by the organic motion of the stomach, which their presence excites. They act on each other by the effect of this juxtaposition and fermentation must take place. All that is nourishing ferments.

In consequence of all of these operations, chyle is elaborated and spread over the food, which then passes the pylorus and enters the intestines. Portion after portion succeeds until the stomach is empty, thus evacuating itself as it was filled.

The pylorus is a kind of chamber between the stomach and the intestines, so constructed that food once in it can ascend only with great difficulty. This viscera is sometimes obstructed when the sufferer, after long and intense agony, dies of hunger.

The next intestine beyond the pylorus is the duodenum. It is so called because it is twelve fingers long.

When chyle reaches the duodenum, it receives a new elaboration by being mingled with bile and the panchreatic juice. It loses the grey color and acidity it previously possessed, becomes yellow and commences to assume a *stercoral* odor, which increases as it advances to the rectum. The various substances act reciprocally on each other; there must, consequently, be many analagous gasses produced.

The impulse which ejected chyle from the stomach, continues and forces the food towards the lower intestines, there the chyle separates itself and is absorbed by organs intended for the purpose, whence it proceeds to the liver, to mingle with the blood, which it revives, and thus repairs the losses of the vital organs and of transpiration.

It is difficult to explain how chyle, which is a light and almost insipid fluid, can be extracted from a mass, the color of which, and the taste, are so deeply pronounced.

Be that as it may, the preparation of chyle appears to be the true object of digestion, and as soon as it mingles with the circulation, the individual becomes aware of a great increase of physical power.

The digestion of fluids is less complicated than that of solids, and can be explained in a few words.

The purely liquid portion is absorbed by the stomach, and thrown into circulation; thence it is taken to the veins by the arteries and filtered by urethras,[33] which pass them as urine, to the bladder.

When in this last receptacle, and though restrained by the spinchter muscle, the urine remains there but a brief time; its exciting nature causes a desire to avoid it, and soon voluntary constriction emits it through canals, which common consent does not permit us to name.

Digestion varies in the time it consumes, according to the temperament of individuals. The mean time, however, is seven hours, *viz.*, three hours for the stomach, and the rest of the time for the lower intestines.

From this exposé which I have selected from the most reliable authors, I have separated all anatomical rigidities, and scientific abstractions. My readers will thence be able to judge where the last meal they ate is: viz., during the first three

---

[33] These urethras are conduits of the size of a pea, which start from the kidneys, and end at the upper neck of the bladder.

hours in the stomach, later in the intestinal canal, and after seven hours, awaiting expulsion.

INFLUENCE OF DIGESTION

Of all corporeal operations, digestion is the one which has the closest connection with the moral condition of man.

This assertion should amaze no one; things cannot be otherwise.

The principles of physiology tells us that the soul is liable to impressions only in proportion as the organs subjected to it have relation to external objects, whence it follows that when these organs are badly preserved, badly restored, or irritated, this state of degradation exerts a necessary influence on sensations, which are the intermediates of mental operations.

Thus the habitual manner in which digestion is performed or affected, makes us either sad, gay, taciturn, gossiping morose or melancholy, without our being able to doubt the fact, or to resist it for a moment.

In this respect, humanity may be arranged under three categories; the regular, the reserved, and the uncertain.

Each of the persons who belong to each of the series, not only have similar dispositions, and propensities, but there is something analogous and similar in the manner in which they fulfill the mission from which chance during their lives has separated them.

To exhibit an example, I will go into the vast field of literature. I think men of letters frequently owe all their characteristics to their peculiar mode of life. Comic poets must be of one kind, tragic poets of another, and elegiac, of the uncertain class. The most elegiac and the most comic are only separated by a variety of digestive functions.

By an application of this principle to courage, when Prince Eugene of Savoy, was doing the greatest injury to France, some one said, "Ah, why can I not send him a *pâté de foie gras*, three times a week I would make him the greatest sluggard of Europe."

"Let us hurry our men into action, while a little beef is left in their bowels," said an English general.

Digestion in the young is very often accompanied by a slight chill, and in the old, by a great wish to sleep. In the first case, nature extracts the coloric from the surface to use it in its laboratory. In the second, the same power debilitated by age cannot at once satisfy both digestion and the excitement of the senses.

When digestion has just begun, it is dangerous to yield to a disposition for mental work. One of the greatest causes of mortality is, that some men after having dined, and perhaps too well dined, can neither close their eyes nor their ears.

This observation contains a piece of advice, which should even attract the most careless youth, usually attentive to nothing. It should also arrest the attention of grown men, who forget nothing, not even that time never pauses, and which is a penal law to those on the wrong side of fifty.

Some persons are fretful while digestion is going on. At that time, nothing should be suggested to and no favors asked of them.

Among these was marshal Augereau, who, during the first hour after dinner, slaughtered friends and enemies indiscriminately.

I have heard it said, that there were two persons in the army, whom the general-in-chief always wished to have shot, the commissary-in-chief and the head of his general staff. They were both present. Cherin the chief of staff, talked back to him, and the commissary, though he said nothing, did not think a bit the less.

At that time, I was attached to his general staff, and always had a plate at his table. I used, however, to go thither rarely, being always afraid of his periodical outbreaks, and that he would send me to dinner to finish my digestion.

I met him afterwards at Paris, and as he testified his regret that he had not seen me oftener, I did not conceal the reason. We laughed over the matter and he confessed that I was not wrong.

We were then at Offenbourg, and a complaint was made by the staff that we ate neither game nor fish.

This complaint was well founded, for it is a maxim, of public law, that the conquerors should always live at the expense of the conquered. On that very day I wrote a letter to the master of the forests to point out a remedy.

This official was an old trooper, who doubtless was unwilling to treat us kindly lest we should take root in this territory. His answer was negative and evasive. The gamekeepers, afraid of our soldiers, had gone, the fishermen were insubordinate, the water muddy, etc. To all this, I said nothing, but I sent him ten grenadiers to be lodged and fed until further orders.

The remedy was effective; for early on the next day after, I saw a heavily loaded wagon come. The gamekeepers had come back, the fishermen were submissive; we had game and fish enough to last for a week.

We had kid, snipe, lark, pike, etc.

When I received the offering, I freed the superintendent from his troublesome guests, and during the whole time we remained in that part of the country, we had nothing to complain of.

MEDITATION XVII

REPOSE

MAN is not made to enjoy an indefinite activity; nature has destined him to a variable existence, and his perceptions must end after a certain time. This time of activity may be prolonged, by varying the nature of the perceptions to be experienced, and a continuity of life brings about a desire for repose.

Repose leads to sleep, and sleep produces dreams.

Here we find ourselves on the very verge of humanity, for the man who sleeps is something more than a mere social being: the law protects, but does not command him.

Here a very singular fact told me by Dom Duhaget, once prior of the Chartreuse convent of Pierre Chatel, presents itself.

Dom Duhaget was a member of a very good family in Gascogne, and had served with some distinction as a captain of infantry. He was a knight of St Louis. I never knew any one, the conversation of whom was more pleasant.

"There was," said he, "before I went to Pierre Chatel, a monk of a very melancholy humor, whose character was very somber, and who was looked upon as a somnambulist.

"He used often to leave his cell, and when he went astray, people were forced to guide him back again. Many attempts had been made to cure him, but in vain.

"One evening I had not gone to bed at the usual hour, but was in my office looking over several papers, when I saw this monk enter in a perfect state of somnambulism.

"His eyes were open but fixed, and he was clad in the tunic in which he should have gone to bed, but he had a huge knife in his hand.

"He came at once to my bed, the position of which he was familiar with, and after having felt my hand, struck three blows which penetrated the mattress on which I laid.

"As he passed in front of me his brows were knit, and I saw an expression of extreme gratification pervaded his face.

"The light of two lamps on my desk made no impression, and he returned as he had come, opening the doors which led to his cell, and I soon became satisfied that he had quietly gone to bed.

"You may," said the Prior, "fancy my state after this terrible apparition; I trembled at the danger I had escaped, and gave thanks to Providence. My emotion, however, was so great that during the balance of the night I could not sleep.

"On the next day I sent for the somnambulist and asked him what he had dreamed of during the preceding night.

"When I asked the question he became troubled. 'Father,' said he, 'I had so strange a dream that it really annoys me; I fear almost to tell you for I am sure the devil has had his hand in it.' 'I order you to tell me,' said I, 'dreams are involuntary and this may only be an illusion. Speak sincerely to me.' 'Father,' said he,' I had scarcely gone to sleep when I dreamed that you had killed my mother, and when her bloody shadow appeared to demand vengeance, I hurried into your cell, and as I thought stabbed you. Not long after I arose, covered with perspiration, and thanked God that I had not committed the crime I had meditated.' 'It has been more nearly committed,' said I, with a kind voice, 'than you think.'

"I then told him what had passed, and pointed out to him the blows he had aimed at me.

"He cast himself at my feet, and all in tears wept over the involuntary crime he had thought to commit, and besought me to inflict any penance I might think fit.

"'No,' said I, 'I will not punish you for an involuntary act. Henceforth, though I excuse you from the service of the night, I inform you that your cell will be locked on the outside and never be opened except to permit you to attend to the first mass.'"

If in this instance, from which a miracle only saved him, the Prior had been killed, the monk would not have suffered, for he would have committed a homicide not a murder.

TIME OF REST

The general laws of the globe we inhabit have an influence on the human race. The alternatives of day and night are felt with certain varieties over the whole globe, but the result of all this is the indication of a season of quiet and repose. Probably we would not have been the same persons had we lived all our lives without any change of day or night.

Be this as it may, when one has enjoyed for a certain length of time a plentitude of life a time comes when he can enjoy nothing; his impressibility gradually decreases, and the effects on each of his senses are badly arranged. The organs are dull and the soul becomes obtuse.

It is easy to see that we have had social man under consideration, surrounded by all the attractions of civilization. The necessity of this is peculiarly evident to all who are buried either in the studio, travel, as soldiers, or in any other manner.

In repose our mother nature especially luxuriates. The man who really reposes, enjoys a happiness which is as general as it is indefinable; his arms sink by their own weight, his fibres distend, his brain becomes refreshed, his senses become calm, and his sensations obtuse. He wishes for nothing, he does not reflect, a veil of gauze is spread before his eyes, and in a few moments he will sink to sleep.

MEDITATION XVIII

SLEEP

THOUGH some men be organized that they may be said not to sleep, yet the great necessity of the want of sleep is well defined as is hunger or thirst. The advanced sentinels of the army used often to sleep though they filled their eyes with snuff.

DEFINITION

Sleep is a physical condition, during which man separates himself from external objects by the inactivity of his senses, and has only a mechanical life.

Sleep, like night, is preceded and followed by two twilights. The one leads to inertion, the other to activity.

Let us seek to elucidate these phenomena.

When sleep begins, the organs of the senses fall almost into inactivity. Taste first disappears, then the sight and smell. The ear still is on the alert, and touch never slumbers. It ever warns us of danger to which the body is liable.

Sleep is always preceded by a more or less voluptuous sensation. The body yields to it with pleasure, being certain of a prompt restoration. The soul gives up to it with confidence, hoping that its means of fiction will he retempered.

From the fact of their not appreciating this sensation, savants of high rank have compared sleep to death, which all living beings resist as much as possible, and which even animals show a horror of.

Like all pleasures, sleep becomes a passion. Persons have been known to sleep away three-quarters of their life. Like all other passions it then exerts the worst influences, producing idleness, indolence, sloth and death.

The school of Salernum granted only seven hours to sleep without distinction to sex or age. This maxim was too severe, for more time is needed by children, and more should, from complaisance, be granted to women. Though whenever more than ten hours is passed in bed there is abuse.

In the early hours of crepuscular sleep, will yet exists. We can rouse ourselves, and the eye has not yet lost all its power. *Non omnibus dormio*, said

Mecenes, and in this state more than one husband has acquired a sad certainty. Some ideas yet originate but are incoherent. There are doubtful lights, and see indistinct forms flit around. This condition does not last long, for sleep soon becomes absolute.

What does the soul do in the interim? It lives in itself, and like a pilot in a calm, like a mirror at night, a lute that no one touches, awakes new excitement.

Some psycologists, among others the count of Redern, say that the soul always acts. The evidence is, that a man aroused from sleep always preserves a memory of his dreams.

There is something in this observation, which deserves verification.

This state of annihilation, however, is of brief duration, never exceeding more than five or six hours: losses are gradually repaired, an obscure sense of existence manifests itself, and the sleeper passes into the empire of dreams.

MEDITATION XIX

DREAMS

Dreams are material impressions on the soul, without the intervention of external objects.

These phenomena, so common in ordinary times, are yet little known.

The fault resides with the *savants* who did not allow us a sufficiently great number of instances. Time will however remedy this, and the double nature of man will be better known.

In the present state of science, it must be taken for granted that there exists a fluid, subtle as it is powerful, which transmits to the brain the impressions received by the senses. This excitement is the cause of ideas.

Absolute sleep is due to the wasted and inertia of this fluid.

We must believe that the labors of digestion and assimilation do not cease during sleep, but repair losses so that there is a time when the individual having already all the necessities of action is not excited by external objects.

Thus the nervous fluid–movable from its nature, passes to the brain, through the nervous conduits. It insinuates itself into the same places, and follows the old road. It produces the same, but less intense effects.

I could easily ascertain the reason of this. When man is impressed by an external object, sensation is sudden, precise, and involuntary. The whole organ is in motion. When on the contrary, the same impression is received in sleep, the posterior portion of the nerves only is in motion, and the sensation is in consequence, less distinct and positive. To make ourselves more easily understood, we will say that when the man is awake, the whole system is impressed, while in sleep, only that portion near the brain is affected.

We know, however, that in voluptuous dreams, nature is almost as much gratified as by our waking sensations; there is, however, this difference in the organs, for each sex has all the elements of gratification.

When the nervous fluid is taken to our brain, it is always collected in vats, so to say, intended for the use of one of our senses, and for that reason, a certain series of ideas, preferable to others, are aroused. Thus we see when the optic nerve is excited, and hear when those of the ear are moved. Let us here remark that taste and smell are rarely experienced in dreams. We dream of flowers, but not of their perfume; we see a magnificently arranged table, but have no perception of the flavor of the dishes.

This is a subject of enquiry worthy of the most distinguished science. We mean, to ascertain why certain senses are lost in sleep, while others preserve almost their full activity. No physiologist has ever taken care of this matter.

Let us remark that the influences we are subject to when we sleep, are internal. Thus, sensual ideas are nothing after the anguish we suffer at a dream of the death of a loved child. At such moments we awake to find ourselves weeping bitterly.

NATURE OF DREAMS

Whimsical as some of the ideas which visit us in dreams may be, we will on examination find they are either recollections, or combinations of memory. I am inclined to say that dreams are the memory of sensations.

Their strangeness exists only in the oddity of association which rejects all idea of law and of chronology, of propriety and time. No one, however, ever dreamed of any thing absolutely unknown to him.

No one will be amazed at the strangeness of our dreams, when we remember, that, when awake, our senses are on the alert, and respectively rectify each other. When a man sleeps, however, every sensation is left to his own resources.

I am inclined to compare these two conditions of the brain, to a piano at which some great musician sits, and who as he throws his fingers over the keys recalls some melody which he might harmonize if he use all his power. This comparison may be extended yet further, when we remember that reflection is to ideas, what harmony is to sounds; that certain ideas contain others, as a principle sound contains the others which follow it, etc. etc.

SYSTEM OF DR. GALL

Having followed thus far a subject which is not without interest, I have come to the confines of the system of Dr. Gall who sustains the multiformity of the organs of the brain.

I cannot go farther, nor pass the limits I have imposed on myself: yet from the love of science, to which it may be seen I am no stranger, I cannot refrain from making known two observations I made with care, and which are the more important, as many persons will be able to verify them.

FIRST OBSERVATION

About 1790 there was in a little village called Gevrin, in the *arrondissement* of Belley a very shrewd tradesman named Landot, who had amassed a very pretty fortune.

All at once he was stricken with paralysis. The Doctors came to his assistance, and preserved his life, not however without loss, for all of his faculties especially memory was gone. He however got on well enough, resumed his appetite and was able to attend to his business.

When seen to be in this state, all those with whom he ever had dealings, thought the time for his revenge was come, and under the pretext of amusing him, offered all kinds of bargains, exchanges, etc. They found themselves mistaken, and had to relinquish their hopes.

The old man had lost none of his commercial faculties. Though he forgot his own name and those of his servants, he was always familiar with the price-current, and knew the exact value of every acre and vineyard in the vicinity.

In this respect his judgment had be en uninjured, and the consequence was, that many of the assailants were taken in their own snares.

SECOND OBSERVATION

At Belley, there was a M. Chirol, who had served for a long time in the *gardes du corps* of Louis XV. and XVI.

He had just sense enough for his profession, but he was passionately fond of all kinds of games, playing l'hombre, piquet, whist, and any new game that from time to time might be introduced.

M. Chirol also became apoplectic and fell into a state of almost absolute insensibility. Two things however were spared, his faculty for digestion, and his passion for play.

He used to go every day to a house he had been used to frequent, sat in a corner and seemed to pay no attention to any thing that passed around him.

When the time came to arrange the card parties, they used to invite him to take a hand. Then it became evident that the malady which had prostrated the majority of his faculties, had not affected his play. Not long before he died, M. Chirol gave a striking proof that this faculty was uninjured.

There came to Belley, a banker from Paris, the name of whom I think was Delins. He had letters of introduction, he was a Parisian, and that was enough in a small city to induce all to seek to make his time pass agreeably as possible.

Delins was a gourmand, and was fond of play. In one point of view he was easily satisfied, for they used to keep him, every day, five or six hours at the table. It was difficult, however, to amuse his second faculty. He was fond of piquet and used to talk of six francs a fiche, far heavier play than we indulged in.

To overcome this obstacle, a company was formed in which each one risked something. Some said that the people of Paris knew more than we; and others that all Parisians were inclined to boasting. The company was however formed, and the game was assigned to M. Chirol.

When the Parisian banker saw the long pale face, and limping form opposed to him, he fancied at first, that he was the butt of joke: when, however, he saw the artistic manner with which the spectre handled the cards, he began to think he had an adversary worthy of him, for once.

He was not slow in being convinced that the faculty yet existed, for not only in that, but in many other games was Delins so beaten that he had to pay more than six hundred francs to the company, which was carefully divided.

RESULT

The consequences of these two observations are easily deduced. It seems clear that in each case, the blow which deranged the brain, had spared for a long time, that portion of the organ employed in commerce and in gaming. It had resisted it beyond doubt, because exercise had given it great power, and because deeply worked impressions hatf exerted great influence on it.

AGE

Age has great influence on the nature of dreams.

In infancy we dream of games, gardens, flowers, and other smiling objects; at a later date, we dream of pleasure, love, battles, and marriages; later still we dream of princely favors, of business, trouble and long departed pleasures.

PHENOMENA OF DREAMS

Certain strange phenomena accompany sleep and dreams. Their study may perhaps account for anthropomania, and for this reason I record here, three observations, selected from a great many made by myself during the silence of night.

FIRST OBSERVATION

I dreamed one night, that I had discovered a means to get rid of the laws of gravitation, so that it became as easy to ascend as descend, and that I could do either as I pleased.

This estate seemed delicious to me; perhaps many persons may have had similar dreams. One curious thing however, occurs to me, which I remember, I explained very distinctly to myself the means which led me to such a result, and they seemed so simple, that I was surprised I had not discovered it sooner.

As I awoke, the whole explanation escaped my mind, but the conclusion remained; since then, I will ever be persuaded of the truth of this observation.

SECOND OBSERVATION

A few months ago while asleep I experienced a sensation of great gratification. It consisted in a kind of delicious tremor of all the organs of which my body was composed, a violet flame played over my brow.

Lambere flamma comas, et circum temporo pasci.

I think this physical state did not last more than twenty seconds, and I awoke with a sensation of something of terror mingled with surprise.

This sensation I can yet remember very distinctly, and from various observations have deduced the conclusion that the limits of pleasure are not, as yet, either known or defined, and that we do not know how far the body may be beatified. I trust that in the course of a few centuries, physiology will explain these sensations and recall them at will, as sleep is produced by opium, and that posterity will be rewarded by them for the atrocious agony they often suffer from when sleeping.

The proposition I have announced, to a degree is sustained by analogy, for I have already remarked that the power of harmony which procures us such acute enjoyments, was totally unknown to the Romans. This discovery is only about five hundred years old.

THIRD OBSERVATION

In the year VIII (1800,) I went to bed as usual and woke up about one, as I was in the habit of doing. I found myself in a strange state of cerebral excitement, my preception was keen, my thoughts profound; the sphere of my intelligence seemed increased, I sat up and my eyes were affected with a pale, vaporous, uncertain light, which, however, did, not enable me to distinguish objects accurately.

Did I only consult the crowd of ideas which succeeded so rapidly, I might have fancied that this state lasted many hours; I am satisfied, however, that it did not last more than half an hour, an external accident, unconnected with volition, however, aroused me from it, and I was recalled to the things of earth.

When the luminous apparition disappeared, I became aware of a sense of dryness, and, in fact, regained my waking faculties. As I was now wide awake, my memory retained a portion of the ideas (indistinctly) which crossed my mind.

The first ideas had time as their subject. It seemed to me that the past, present and future, became identical, were narrowed down to a point, so that it was as easy to look forward into the future, as back into the past. This is all I remember of this first intuition, which was almost effaced by subsequent ones.

Attention was then directed to the senses, which I followed in the order of their perfection, and fancying that those should be examined which were internal as well as external, I began to follow them out.

I found three, and almost four, when I fell again to earth.

1. Compassion is a sensation we feel about the heart when we see another suffer.

2. Predilection is a feeling which attracts us not only to an object, but to all connected with it.

3. Sympathy is the feeling which attracts two beings together.

From the first aspect, one might believe that these two sentiments are one, and the same. They cannot, however, be confounded; for predilection is not always reciprocal, while sympathy, must be.

While thinking of compassion, I was led to a deduction I think very just, and which at another time I would have overlooked. It is the theory on which all legislation is founded.

DO AS YOU WILL BE DONE BY

Alteri ne facias, quod tibi fieri non vis.

Such is an idea of the state in which I was, and to enjoy it again, I would willingly relinquish a month of my life.

In bed we sleep comfortably, in a horizontal position and with the head warm: Thoughts and ideas come quickly and abundantly; expressions follow, and as to write one has to get up, we take off the night cap and go to the desk.

Things all at once seem to change. The examination becomes cold, the thread of our ideas is broken; we are forced to look with trouble, for what was found so easily, and we are often forced to postpone study to another day.

All this is easily explained by the effect produced on the brain by a change of position. The influence of the physic and moral is here experienced.

Following out this observation, I have perhaps gone rather far, but I have been induced to think that the excitability of oriental nations, was, in a manner, due to the fact, that, in obedience to the religion of Mahomet, they used to keep the head warm, for a reason exactly contrary to that which induced all monastic legislators to enjoin shaven crowns.

MEDITATION XX

INFLUENCE OF DIET ON REST, SLEEP AND DREAMS

WHETHER man sleeps, eats, or dreams, he is yet subject to the laws of nutrition and to gastronomy.

Theory and experience, both admit that the quantity and quality of food have a great influence on our repose, rest, and dreams.

EFFECTS OF DIET ON LABOR

A man who is badly fed, cannot bear for a long time, the fatigues of prolonged labor; his strength even abandons him, and to him rest is only loss of power.

If his labor be mental, his ideas are crude and undecided. Reflection contributes nothing to them, nor does judgment analyze them. The brain exhausts itself in vain efforts and the actor slumbers on the battlefield.

I always thought that the suppers of Auteuil and those of the hotels of Rambouillet and Soissons, formed many of the authors of the reign of Louis XIV. Geoffrey was not far wrong when he characterised the authors of the latter part of the eighteenth century as *eau sucrée*. That was their habitual beverage.

According to these principles, I have examined the works of certain well known authors said to have been poor and suffering, and I never found any energy in, them, except when they were stimulated by badly conceived envy.

On the eve of his departure for Boulogne, the Emperor Napoleon fasted for thirty hours, both with his council and with the various depositories of his power, without any refreshment other than two very brief meals, and a few cups of coffee.

Brown, mentions an admiralty clerk, who, having lost his memorandum, without which he could not carry on his duty, passed fifty-two consecutive hours in preparing them again. Without due regimen, he never could have borne the fatigue and sustained himself as follows:—At first, he drank water, then wine, and ultimately took opium.

I met one day a courier, whom I had known in the army, on his way from Spain, whither he had been sent with a government dispatch. (*Correo ganando horas.*)

He made the trip in twelve days, having halted only four hours in Madrid, to drink a few glasses of wine, and to take some soup. This was all the nourishment he took during this long series of sleepless nights and fatigues. He said that more solid sustenance would have made it impossible for him to continue his journey.

DREAMS

Diet has no trifling influence on sleep and dreams.

A hungry man cannot sleep, for the pain he suffers keeps him awake. If weakness or exhaustion overcome him, his slumber is light, uneasy and broken.

A person, however, who has eaten too much, sinks at once to sleep. If he dreams, he remembers nothing of it, for the nervous fluid has been intercepted in the passages. He awakes quickly, and when awake is very sensible of the pains of digestion.

We may then lay down, as a general rule, that coffee rejects sleep. Custom weakens and even causes this inconvenience entirely to disappear. Europeans, whenever they yield to it, always feel its power. Some food, however, gently invites sleep; such as that which contains milk, the whole family of letuces, etc., etc.

CONSEQUENCE

Experience relying on a multitude of observations, has informed us that diet has an influence on dreams.

In general, all stimullkt food excites dreams, such as flock game, ducks, venison and hare.

This quality is recognised in asparagus, celery, truffles, perfume, confectioneries and vanilla.

It would be a great mistake to think that we should banish from our tables all somniferous articles. The dreams they produce are in general agreeable, light, and prolong our existence even when it is suspended.

There are persons to whom sleep is a life apart, and whose dreams are serial, so that they end in one night a dream begun on the night before. While asleep they distinguish faces they remember to have seen, but which they never met with in the real world.

RESULT

A person who reflects on his physical life and who does so according to the principles we develop, is the one who prepares sagaciously for rest, sleep and dreams.

He distributes his labor so that he never over-tasks himself, he lightens it and refreshes himself by brief intervals of rest, which relieve him, without interrupting its continuity, sometimes a duty.

If longer rest is required during the day, he indulges in it only in a sitting attitude; he refuses sleep unless he be forced irresistibly to use it, and is careful not to make it habitual.

When night brings about the hour of repose, he retires to an airy room, does not wrap himself up in curtains, which make him breathe the same air again and again, and never closes the blinds so that when he wakes he will meet with at least one ray of light.

He rests in a bed with the head slightly higher than the feet. His pillow is of hair; his night cap of cloth and his breast unincumbered by a mass of coverings; he is careful, however, to keep his feet warm.

He eats with discretion, and never refuses good and excellent cheer. He drinks prudently, even the best wine. At dessert he talks of gallantry more than of politics, makes more madrigals than epigrams. He takes his coffee, if it suits his constitution, and afterwards swallows a spoonful of liquor, though it he only to perfume his breath. He is, in all respects, a good guest, and yet never exceeds the limits of discretion.

In this state, satisfied with himself and others, he lies down and sinks to sleep. Mysterious dreams then give an agreeable life; he sees those he loves, indulges in his favorite occupations, and visits places which please him.

Then he feels his slumber gradually pass away, and does not regret the time he has lost, because even in his sleep, he has enjoyed unmixed pleasure and an activity without a particle of fatigue.

MEDITATION XXI

OBESITY

Were I a physician with a diploma, I would have written a whole book on obesity; thus I would have acquired a domicil in the domain of science, and would have had the double satisfaction of having, as patients, persons who were perfectly well, and of being besieged by the fairer portion of humanity. To have exactly fat enough, not a bit too much, or too little, is the great study of women of every rank and grade.

What I have not done, some other person will do, and if he be learned and prudent, (and at the same time a good-fellow,) I foretell that he will have wonderful success.

Exoriare aliquis nostris ex ossibus hoeres!

In the intereim, I intend to prepare the way for him. A chapter on obesity is a necessary concomitant of a book which relates so exclusively to eating.

Obesity is that state of greasy congestion in which without the sufferer being sick, the limbs gradually increase in volume, and lose their form and harmony.

One kind of obesity is restricted to the stomach, and I have never observed it in women. Their fibres are generally softer, and when attacked with obesity nothing is spared. I call this variety of obesity GASTROPHORIA. Those attacked by it, I call GASTROPHOROUS. I belong to this category, yet, though my stomach is rather prominent, I have a round and well turned leg. My sinews are like those of an Arab horse.

I always, however, looked on my stomach as a formidable enemy: I gradually subdued it, but after a long contest. I am indebted for all this to a strife of thirty years.

I will begin my treatise by an extract from a collection of more than five hundred dialogues, which at various times I have had with persons menaced with obesity.

AN OBESE.–What delicious bread! where do you get it?

I.–From Limet, in the Rue Richelieu, baker to their Royal Highness, the Due d'Orleans, and the Prince de Conde. I took it from him because he was my neighbour, and have kept to him because he is the best bread maker in the world.

OBESE.–I will remember the address. I eat a great deal of bread, and with such as this could do without any dinner.

OBESE No. 2.–What are you about? You are eating your soup, but set aside the Carolina rice it contains! I.–Ah: that it is a regimen I subject myself to.

OBESE.–It is a bad regimen. I am fond of rice pâtés and all such things. Nothing is more nourishing.

AN IMMENSE OBESE.–Do me the favor to pass me the potatoes before you. They go so fast that I fear I shall not be in time.

I.–There they are, sir.

OBESE.–But you will take some? There are enough for two, and after us the deluge.

I.–Not I. I look on the potatoe as a great preservative against famine; nothing, however, seems to me so pre-eminently *fade.*

OBESE.–That is a gastronomical heresy. Nothing is better than the potatoe; I eat them in every way.

AN OBESE LADY.–Be pleased to send me the Soissons haricots I see at the other end of the table.

I.–(*Having obeyed the order, hummed in a low tone, the well known air:*)

"Les Soissonnais sont heureux, Les haricots sont chez eux."

OBESE.–Do not laugh: it is a real treasure for this country. Paris gains immensely by it. I will thank you to pass me the English peas. When young they are food fit for the gods.

I?–Anathema on beans and peas.

OBESE.–Bah, for your anathema; you talk as if you were a whole council.

I.–(*To another.*) I congratulate you on your good health, it seems to me that you have fattened somewhat, since I last saw you.

OBESE.–I probably owe it to a change of diet.

I.–How so?

OBESE.–For some time I eat a rich soup for breakfast, and so thick that the spoon would stand up in it.

I.–(*To another.*) Madame, if I do not mistake, you will accept a portion of this charlotte? I will attack it.

OBESE.–No, sir. I have two things which I prefer. This gateau of rice and that Savoy biscuit–I am very fond of sweet things.

I.–While they talk politics, madame, at the other end of the table, will you take a piece of this *tourte a la frangipane*?

OBESE.–Yes; I like nothing better than pastry. We have a pastry- cook in our house as a lodger, and I think my daughter and I eat up all his rent.

I.–(*Looking at the daughter.*) You both are benefitted by the diet. Your daughter is a fine looking young woman.

OBESE LADY.–Yes; but there are persons who say she is too fat.

I.–Ah! those who do so are envious, etc., etc. By this and similar conversations I elucidate a theory I have formed about the human race, viz: Greasy corpulence always has, as its first cause, a diet with too much farinacious or feculent substance. I am sure the same regime will always have the same effect. Carniverous animals never become fat. One has only to look at the wolf, jackal, lion, eagle, etc.

Herbiverous animals do not either become fat until age has made repose a necessity. They, however, fatten quickly when fed on potatoes, farinacious grain, etc.

Obesity is rarely met with among savage nations, or in that class of persons who eat to live, instead of living to eat.

CAUSES OF OBESITY

From the preceding observation, the causes of which any one may verify, it is easy to ascertain the principle causes of obesity.

The first is the nature of the individual. Almost all men are born with predispositions, the impress of which is borne by their faces. Of every hundred persons who die of diseases of the chest, ninety have dark hair, long faces and sharp noses. Of every hundred obese persons, ninety have short faces, blue eyes, and pug noses.

Then there are beyond doubt persons predestined to obesity, the digestive powers of whom elaborate a great quantity of grease.

This physical fact, of the truth of which I am fully satisfied, exerts a most important influence on our manner of looking at things.

When we meet in society, a short, fat, rosy, short-nosed individual, with round limbs, short feet, etc., all pronounce her charming. Better informed than others, however, I anticipate the ravages which ten years will have effected on her, and sigh over evils which as yet do not exist. This anticipated compassion is a painful sentiment, and proves that a prescience of the future would only make man more unhappy.

The second of the causes of obesity, is the fact that farinacious and feculaferous matter is the basis of our daily food. We have already said that all animals that live on farinaceous substances become fat; man obeys the common law.

The fecula is more prompt in its action when it is mingled with sugar. Sugar and grease are alike in containing large quantities of hydrogen, and are both inflammable. This combination is the more powerful, from the fact that it flatters the taste, and that we never eat sweet things until the appetite is already satisfied, so that we are forced to court the luxury of eating by every refinement of temptation.

The fecula is not less fattening when in solution, as in beer, and other drinks of the same kind. The nations who indulge the most in them, are those who have the most huge stomachs. Some Parisian families who in 1817 drank beer habitually, because of the dearness of wine, were rewarded by a degree of embonpoint, they would be glad to get rid of.

SEQUEL

Another cause of obesity is found in the prolongation of sleep, and want of exercise. The human body repairs itself much during sleep, and at the same time loses nothing, because muscular action is entirely suspended. The acquired superfluity must then be evaporated by exercise.

Another consequence is, that persons who sleep soundly, always refuse every thing that looks the least like fatigue. The excess of assimilation is then borne away by the torrent of circulation. It takes possession, by a process, the secret of which nature has reserved to herself, of some hundredths of hydrogen, and fat is formed to be deposited in the tubes of the cellular tissue.

SEQUEL

The last cause of obesity is excess of eating and drinking.

There was justice in the assertion, that one of the privileges of the human race is to eat without hunger, and drink without thirst. Animals cannot have it, for it arises from reflection on the pleasures of the table, and a desire to prolong its duration.

This double passion has been found wherever man exists. We know savages eat to the very acme of brutality, whenever they have an opportunity.

Cosmopolites, as citizens of two hemispheres, we fancy ourselves at the very apogee of civilization, yet we are sure we eat too much.

This is not the case with the few, who from avarice or want of power, live alone. The first are delighted at the idea that they amass money, and others distressed that they do not. It is the case, however, with those around us, for all, whether hosts or guests, offer and accept with complaisance.

This cause, almost always present, acts differently, according to the constitution of individuals; and in those who have badly organized stomachs, produces indigestion, but not obesity.

ANECDOTE

This one instance, which all Paris will remember.

M. Lang had one of the most splendid establishments of the capital; his table especially, was excellent, but his digestion was bad as his gourmandise was great. He did the honors with perfect taste, and ate with a resolution worthy of a better fate.

All used to go on very well, till coffee was introduced, but the stomach soon refused the labor to which it had been subjected, and the unfortunate gastronomer was forced to throw himself on the sofa and remain in agony until the next day, in expiation of the brief pleasure he had enjoyed.

It is very strange that he never corrected this fault: as long as he lived, he was subjected to this alternative, yet the sufferings of the evening never had any influence on the next days' meal.

Persons with active digestion, fare as was described in the preceding article. All is digested, and what is not needed for nutrition is fixed and turned into fat.

Others have a perpetual indigestion, and food is passed without having left any nourishment. Those who do not understand the matter, are amazed that so many good things do not produce a better effect.

It may be seen that I do not go very minutely into the matter, for from our habits many secondary causes arise, due to our habits, condition, inclinations, pleasures, etc.

I leave all this to the successor I pointed out in the commencement of this work, and satisfy myself merely with the prelibation, the right of the first comer to every sacrifice.

Intemperance has long attracted the attention of observers. Princes have made sumptuary laws, religion has moralized for gourmandise, but, alas, a mouthfull less was never eaten, and the best of eating every day becomes more flourishing.

I would perhaps be fortunate in the adoption of a new course, and in the exposition of the physical causes of obesity. Self- preservation would perhaps be more powerful than morals, or persuasive than reason, have more influence than laws, and I think the fair sex would open their eyes to the light.

INCONVENIENCE OF OBESITY

Obesity has a lamentable influence on the two sexes, inasmuch as it is most injurious to strength and beauty.

It lessens strength because it increases the weight to be moved, while the motive power is unchanged. It injures respiration, and makes all labor requiring prolonged muscular power impossible.

Obesity destroys beauty by annihilating the harmony of primitive proportions, for all the limbs do not proportionately fatten.

It destroys beauty by filling up cavities nature's hand itself designed.

Nothing is so common as to see faces, once very interesting, made commonplacc by obesity.

The head of the last government did not escape this law. Towards the latter portion of his life, he (Napoleon) became bloated, and his eyes lost a great portion of their expression.

Obesity produces a distaste for dancing, walking, riding, and an inaptitude for those amusements which require skill or agility.

It also creates a disposition to certain diseases, such as apoplexy, dropsy, ulcers in the legs, and makes all diseases difficult to cure.

EXAMPLES OF OBESITY

I can remember no corpulent heroes except Marius and John Sobieski.

Marius was short, and was about as broad as he was long. That probably frightened the Cimber who was about to kill him.

The obesity of the King of Poland had nearly been fatal to him, for having stumbled on a squadron of Turkish cavalry, from which he had to fly, he would certainly have been massacred, if his aids had not sustained him, almost fainting from fatigue on his horse, while others generously sacrificed themselves to protect him.

If I am not mistaken, the Duc de Vendome, a worthy son of Henry IV., was also very corpulent. He died at an inn, deserted by all, and preserved consciousness just long enough to see a servant snatch away a pillow on which his head was resting.

There are many instances of remarkable obesity. I will only speak, however, of my own observations.

M. Rameau, a fellow student of mine and *maire* of Chaleur, was about five feet two inches high, but weighed five hundred pounds.

The Duc de Luynes, beside whom I often sat, became enormous. Fat had effaced his handsome features, and he slept away the best portion of his life.

The most remarkable case, though, I saw in New York, and many persons now in Paris will remember to have seen at the door of a café in Broadway, a person seated in an immense arm-chair, with legs stout enough to have sustained a church.[34]

Edward was at least five feet ten inches, and was about eight feet (French) in circumference. His fingers were like those of the Roman Emperor, who used to wear his wife's bracelets as rings. His arms and legs were nearly as thick as the waist of a man of medium size, and his feet were elephantine, covered by fat

---

[34] Many persons in New York remember the person referred to. The translator has heard, that as late as 1815, he was frequently to be seen at the door of a house near where the Atheneum Hotel was. Brillat Savarin is said scarcely to exaggerate.

pendant from his legs. The fat on his cheek had weighed down his lower eye-lid, and three hanging chins made his face horrible to behold.

He passed his life near a window, which looked out on the street and drank from time to time a glass of ale from a huge pitcher he kept by his side.

His strange appearance used to attract the attention of passers, whom he used always to put to flight by saying in a sepulchral tone "What are you staring at like wild cats? Go about your business, you blackguards," etc.

Having spoken to him one day, he told me that he was not at all annoyed and that if death did not interrupt him, he would be glad to live till the day of judgment.

From the preceding, it appears that if obesity be not a disease, it is at least a very troublesome predisposition, into which we fall from our own fault.

The result is, that we should all seek to preserve ourselves from it before we are attacked, and to cure ourselves when it befalls us. For the sake of the unfortunate we will examine what resources science presents us.

MEDITATION XXII

PRESERVATIVE TREATMENT AND CURE OF OBESITY.[35]

I WILL begin by a fact which proves that courage is needed not only to prevent but to cure obesity.

M. Louis Greffulhe, whom his majesty afterwards honored with the title of count, came one morning to see me, saying that he had understood that I had paid great attention to obesity, and asked me for advice.

"Monsieur," said I, "not being a doctor with a diploma, I might refuse you, but I will not, provided you give me your word of honor that for one month you will rigorously obey my directions."

M. Greffulhe made the promise I required and gave me his hand. On the next day, I gave him my directions, the first article of which demanded that he should at once get himself weighed, so that the result might be made mathematically.

After a month he came to see me again, and spoke to me nearly thus:

"Monsieur," said he, "I followed your prescription as if my life depended on it, and during the month I am satisfied that I have lost three pounds and more; but have for that purpose to violate all my tastes and, habits so completely, that while I thank you for your advice I must decline to follow it, and await quietly the fate God ordains for me."

I heard this resolution with pain. M. Greffulhe became every day fatter and subject to all the inconveniences of extreme obesity, and died of suffocation when he was about forty.

GENERALITIES

The cure of obesity should begin with three precepts of absolute theory, discretion in eating, moderation in sleep, and exercise on foot or horseback.

---

[35] About twenty years ago I began a treatise, *ex professo*, on obesity. My readers must especially regret the preface which was of dramatic form. I averred to a physician that a fever is less dangerous than a law suit; for the latter, after having made a man run, fatigue, and worry himself, strips him of pleasure, money, and life. This is a statement which might be propagated as well as any other.

These are the first resources presented to us by science. I, however, have little faith in them, for I know men and things enough to be aware that any prescription, not literally followed, has but a light effect.

Now, imprimus, it needs much courage to be able to leave the table hungry. As long as the want of food is felt, one mouthful makes the succeeding one more palatable, and in general as long as we are hungry, we eat in spite of doctors, though in that respect we follow their example.

In the second place to ask obese persons to rise early is to stab them to the heart. They will tell you that their health will not suffer them, that when they rise early they are good for nothing all day. Women will plead exhaustion, will consent to sit up late, and wish to fatten on the morning's nap. They lose thus this resource.

In the third place, riding as an exercise is expensive, and does not suit every rank and fortune.

Propose this to a female patient and she will consent with joy, provided she have a gentle but active horse, a riding dress in the height of the fashion, and in the third place a squire who is young, good-tempered and handsome. It is difficult to fill these three requisites, and riding is thus given up.

Exercise on foot is liable to many other objections. It is fatiguing, produces perspiration and pleurisy. Dust soils the shoes and stockings, and it is given up. If, too, the patient have the least headache, if a single shot, though no larger than the head of a pin, pierce the skin it is all charged to the exercise.

The consequence is that all who wish to diminish embonpoint should eat moderately, sleep little, and take as much exercise as possible, seeking to accomplish the purpose in another manner. This method, based on the soundest principles of physics and chemistry, consists in a diet suited to the effects sought for.

Of all medical powers, diet is the most important, for it is constant by night and day, whether waking or sleeping. Its effect is renewed at every meal, and gradually exerts its influence on every portion of the individual. The antiobesic regimen is therefore indicated by the most common causes of the diseases, and by the fact that it has been shown that farina or fecula form fat in both men and animals. In the latter, the case is evident every day, and from it we may deduce the conclusion that obtaining from farinaceous food will be beneficial.

But my readers of both sexes will exclaim, "Oh my God, how cruel the professor is. He has at once prescribed all we like, the white rolls of Limet, the biscuit of Achard. the cakes of ... and all the good things made with sugar, eggs, and farina. He will spare neither potatoes nor macaroni. Who would have expected it from a man fond of everything good?"

"What is that?" said I, putting on my stern look which I call up but once a year. "Well, eat and grow fat, become ugly, asthmatic and die of melted fat. I will make a note of your case and you shall figure in my second edition. Ah! I see, one phrase has overcome you, and you beg me to suspend the thunderbolt. Be easy, I will prescribe your diet and prove how much pleasure is in the grasp of one who lives to eat."

"You like bread? well, eat barley-bread. The admirable Cadet de Vaux long ago extolled its virtues. It is not so nourishing and not so agreeable. The precept will then be more easily complied with. To be sure one should resist temptation. Remember this, which is a principle of sound morality.

"You like soup? Eat *julienne* then, with green vegetables, with cabbage and roots. I prohibit *soup au pain*, *pâtés* and *purees*.

"Eat what you please at the first course except rice *aux volailles* and the crust of *pâtés*. Eat well, but circumspectly.

"The second course will call for all your philosophy. Avoid everything farinacious, under whatever form it appears. You have yet the roasts, salads, and herbacious vegetables.

"Now for the dessert. This is a new danger, but if you have acted prudently so far, you may survive it. Avoid the head of the table, where things that are dangerous to you are most apt to appear. Do not look at either biscuits or macaronies; you have fruits of all kinds, confitures and much else that you may safely indulge in, according to my principles.

"After dinner I prescribe coffee, permit you *liqueurs*, and advise you to take tea and punch.

"At breakfast barly-bread is a necessity, and take chocolate rather than coffee. I, however, permit strong *café au lait*. One cannot breakfast too soon. When we breakfast late, dinner time comes before your digestion is complete. You eat though, and eating without appetite is often a great cause of obesity, when we do so too often."

SEQUEL OF THE REGIMEN

So far I have, like a tender father, marked out a regimen which will prevent obesity. Let us add a few remarks about its cure.

Drink every summer thirty bottles of Seltzer water, a large glass in the morning, two before breakfast and another at bedtime. Drink light white acid wines like those of Anjon. Avoid beer as you would the plague. Eat radishes, artichokes, asparagus, etc. Eat lamb and chicken in preference to other animal food; eat only the crust of bread, and employ a doctor who follows my principles, and as soon as you begin you will find yourself fresher, prettier, and better in every respect.

Having thus placed you ashore, I must point out the shoals, lest in excess or zeal, you overleap the mark.

The shoal I wish to point out is the habitual use made by some stupid people of acids, the bad effects of which experience has demonstrated.

DANGERS OF ACIDS

There is a current opinion among women, which every year causes the death of many young women, that acids, especially vinegar, are preventives of obesity. Beyond all doubts, acids have the effect of destroying obesity, but they also destroy health and freshness. Lemonade is of all acids the most harmless, but few stomachs can resist it long.

The truth I wish to announce cannot be too public, and almost all of my readers can bring forward some fact to sustain it.

I knew in 1776, at Dijon, a young lady of great beauty, to whom I was attached by bonds of friendship, great almost as those of love. One day when she had for some time gradually grown pale and thin (previously she had a delicious *embonpoint*) she told me in confidence that as her young friends had ridiculed her for being too fat, she had, to counteract the tendency, been in the habit every day of drinking a large glass of *vinaigre*.

I shuddered at the confession, and made every attempt to avoid the danger. I informed her mother of the state of things the next day, and as she adored her daughter, she was as much alarmed as I was. The doctors were sent for, but in vain, for before the cause of her malady was suspected, it was incurable and hopeless.

Thus, in consequence of having followed imprudent advice, our amiable Louise was led to the terrible condition of marasmus, and sank when scarcely eighteen years old, to sleep forever.

She died casting longing looks towards a future, which to her would have no existence, and the idea that she had involuntarily attempted her own life, made her existence more prompt and painful.

I have never seen any one else die; she breathed her last in my arms, as I lifted her up to enable her to see the day. Eight days after her death, her broken hearted mother wished me to visit with her the remains of her daughter, and we saw an extatic appearance which had not hitherto been visible. I was amazed, but extracted some consolation from the fact. This however is not strange, for Lavater tells of many such in his history of physiogomy.

ANTIOBESIC BELT

All antiobesic tendencies should be accompanied by a precaution I had forgotten. It consists in wearing night and day, a girdle to repress the stomach, by moderately clasping it.

To cause the necessity of it to be perceived, we must remember that the vertebral column, forming one of the walls in the cavity containing the intestines, is firm and inflexible. Whence it follows, that the excess of weight which intestines acquire as soon as obesity causes them to deviate from the vertical line, rests on the envelopes which compose the skin of the stomach. The latter being susceptible of almost infinite distention, would be unable to replace themselves, when this effort diminishes, if they did not have a mechanical art, which, resting on the dorsal column, becomes an antagonist, and restores equilibrium. This belt has therefore the effect of preventing the intestines from yielding to their actual weight, and gives a power to contract when pressure is diminished. It should never be laid aside, or the benefit it exerts in the day will be destroyed in the night. It is not, however, in the least troublesome, and one soon becomes used to it.

The belt also shows when we have eaten enough; and it should be made with great care, and so contrived as to diminish as the *embonpoint* decreases.

One is not forced to wear it all life long, and it may be laid aside when the inconvenience is sufficiently reduced. A suitable diet however, should be maintained. I have not worn it for six years.

QUINQUINA

One substance I think decidedly antiobesic. Many observations have induced me to think so, yet I leave the matter in doubt, and submit it to physicians.

This is quinquina.

Ten or twelve persons that I know, have had long intermittent fevers; some were cured by old women's remedies, powders, etc. Others by the continued use of quinquina, which is always effective.

All those persons of the same category, gradually regained their obesity. Those of the second, lost their *embonpoint*, a circumstance which leaves me to think the quinquina which produced the last result had the effect I speak of.

Rational theory is not opposed to this deduction, for quinquina, exciting all the vital powers, may give the circulation an impetus which troubles all, and dissipates, the gas destined to become fat. It is also shown that quinquina contains a portion of tannin which is powerful enough to close the cells which contain grease. It is possible that these two effects sustain each other.

These two ideas, the truth of which any one may understand, induce me to recommend quinquina to all those who wish to get rid of troublesome *embonpoint*. Thus *dummodo annuerit in omni medicationis genere doctissimi Facultatis professores*. I think that after the first month of any regimen, the person who wishes to get rid of fat, should take every day before breakfast, a glass of white wine, in which was placed a spoonful of coffee and red quinquina. Such are the means I suggest to overcome a very troublesome affection. I have accommodated them to human weakness and to our manners.

In this respect the experimental truth is relied on, which teaches that in proportion as a regime is vigorous, it is dangerous, for he who does not follow it literally, does not follow it all.

Great efforts are rare, and if one wishes to be followed, men must be offered things vacile, if not agreeable.

Jean Anthelme Brillat-Savarin

MEDITATION XXIII

THINNESS

DEFINITION

THINNESS is the state of that individual, the muscular frame of whom is not filled up by strength, and who exhibits all angles of the long scaffolding.

VARIETIES

There are two kinds of thinness; the first is the result of the primitive disposition of the body, and is accompanied by health, and a full use of the organic functions of the body. The second is caused by the fact that some of the organs are more defective than others, and give the individual an unhappy and miserable appearance. I once knew young woman of moderate stature who only weighed sixty-five pounds.

EFFECTS OF THINNESS

Thinness is a matter of no great trouble to men. They have no less strength, and are far more active. The father of the young woman I spoke of, though, very thin, could seize a chair by his teeth and throw it over his head.

It is, however, a terrible misfortune to women, to whom beauty is more important than life, and the beauty of whom consists in the roundness and graceful contour of their forms. The most careful toilette, the most, sublime needle-work, cannot hide certain deficiencies. It has been said that whenever a pin is taken from a thin woman, beautiful as she may be, she loses some charm.

The thin have, therefore, no remedy, except from the interference of the faculty. The regimen must be so long, that the cure must be slow.

Women, however, who are thin, and who have a good stomach, are found to be as susceptible of fat as chickens. A little time, only, is necessary, for the stomach of chickens is comparatively smaller, and they cannot be submitted to as regular a diet as chickens are.

This is the most gentle comparison which suggested itself to me. I needed one, and ladies will excuse me for the reason for which I wrote this chapter.

NATURAL PREDESTINATION

Nature varies its works, and has remedies for thinness, as it has for obesity.

Persons intended to be thin are long drawn out. They have long hands and feet, legs thin, and the *os coxigis* retroceding. Their sides are strongly marked, their noses prominent, large mouths, sharp chins and brown hair.

This is the general type, the individual elements may sometimes vary; this however happens rarely.

Thin people sometimes eat a great deal. All I ever even talked with, confess that they digest badly. That is the reason they remain thin.

They are of every class and temperament. Some have nothing salient either in feature or in form. Their eyes are inexpressive, their lips pale, and every feature denotes a want of energy, weakness, and something like suffering. One might almost say they seemed to be incomplete, and that the torch of their lives had not been well lighted.

FATTENING REGIMEN

All thin women wish to be fat; this is a wish we have heard expressed a thousand times. To render, then, this last homage to the powerful sex, we seek to replace by folds of silk and cotton, exposed in fashion shops, to the great scandal of the severe, who turn aside, and look away from them, as they would from chimeras, more carefully than if the reality presented themselves to their eyes.

The whole secret of *embonpoint* consists in a suitable diet. One need only eat and select suitable food.

With this regimen, our disposition to sleep is almost unimportant. If you do not take exercise, you will be exposed to fatness. If you do, you will yet grow fat.

If you sleep much, you will grow fat, if you sleep little, your digestion will increase, and you will eat more.

We have then only to speak of the manner they who wish to grow fat should live. This will not be difficult, according to the many directions we have laid down.

To resolve this problem, we must offer to the stomach food which occupies, but does not fatigue it, and displays to the assimilant power, things they can turn into fat.

Let us seek to trace out the daily diet of a sylph, or a sylph disposed to materialize itself.

GENERAL RULE. Much fresh bread will be eaten during the day, and particular care will be taken not to throw away the crumbs.

Before eight in the morning, *soup au pain* or *aux pâtés* will be taken, and afterwards a cup of good chocolate.

At eleven o'clock, breakfast on fresh broiled eggs, *petit pâtés côtelettes*, and what you please; have eggs, coffee will do no harm.

Dinner hour should be so arranged that one should have thoroughly digested before the time comes to sit down at the table. The eating of one meal before another is digested, is an abuse.

After dinner there should be some exercise; men as much as they can; women should go into the Tuilleries, or as they say in America, go shopping. We are satisfied that the little gossip and conversation they maintain is very healthful.

At times, all should take as much soup, potage, fish, etc., and also meat cooked with rice and macaronies, pastry, creams, etc.

At dessert such persons should eat Savoy biscuits, and other things made up of eggs, fecula, and sugar.

This regimen, though apparently circumscribed, is yet susceptible of great variety: it admits the whole animal kingdom, and great care is necessarily taken in the seasoning and preparation of the food presented. The object of this is to prevent disgust, which prevents any amelioration.

Beer should be preferred–if not beer, wines from Bordeaux or from the south of France.

One should avoid all acids, except salads. As much sugar as possible should be put on fruits and all should avoid cold baths. One should seek as long as possible, to breathe the pure country air, eat many grapes when they are in season, and never go to the ball for the mere pleasure of dancing.

Ordinarily one should go to bed about eleven, P. M., and never, under any circumstances, sit up more than an hour later.

Following this regime resolutely, all the distractions of nature will soon be repaired. Health and beauty will both be advanced, and accents of gratitude will ring in the ears of the professor.

Sheep are fattened, as are oxen, lobsters and oysters. Hence, I deduce the general maxim; viz: "He that eats may be made fat, provided that the food be chosen correctly, and according to the physiology of the animal to be fattened."

MEDITATION XXIV

FASTING

DEFINITION

FASTING is a moral abstinence from food, from some religious or moral influence.

Though contrary to our tastes and habits, it is yet of the greatest antiquity.

ORIGIN

Authors explain the matter thus:

In individual troubles, when a father, mother, or beloved child has died, the entire household is in mourning. The body is washed, perfumed, embalmed, and buried as it should be—none then think of eating, but all fast.

In public calamites, when a general drought appears, and cruel wars, or contagious maladies come, we humble ourselves before the power that sent them, and mortify ourselves by abstinence. Misfortune ceases. We become satisfied that the reason was that we fasted, and we continue to have reference to such conjectures.

Thus it is, men afflicted with public calamities or private ones, always yield to sadness, fail to take food, and in the end, make a voluntary act, a religious one.

They fancied they should macerate their body when their soul was oppressed, that they could excite the pity of the gods. This idea seized on all nations and filled them with the idea of mourning, prayers, sacrifice, abstinence, mortification, etc.

Christ came and sanctified fasting. All Christian sects since then have adopted fasting more or less, as an obligation.

HOW PEOPLE USED TO FAST

The practice of fasting, I am sorry to say, has become very rare; and whether for the education of the wicked, or for their conversion, I am glad to tell how we fast now in the XVIII century.

Ordinarily we breakfast before nine o'clock, on bread, cheese, fruit and cold meats.

Between one and two P. M., we take soup or *pot au feu* according to our positions.

About four, there is a little lunch kept up for the benefit of those people who belong to other ages, and for children.

About eight there was a regular supper, with *entrées rôti entremets dessert*: all shared in it, and then went to bed.

In Paris there are always more magnificent suppers, which begin just after the play. The persons who usually attend them are pretty women, admirable actresses, financiers, and men about town. There the events of the day were talked of, the last new song was sung, and politics, literature, etc., were discussed. All persons devoted themselves especially to making love.

Let us see what was done on fast days:

No body breakfasted, and therefore all were more hungry than usual.

All dined as well as possible, but fish and vegetables are soon gone through with. At five o'clock all were furiously hungry, looked at their watches and became enraged, though they were securing their soul's salvation.

At eight o'clock they had not a good supper, but a collation, a word derived from *cloister*, because at the end of the day the monks used to assemble to comment on the works of the fathers, after which they were allowed a glass of wine.

Neither butter, eggs, nor anything animal was served at these collations. They had to be satisfied with salads, confitures, and meats, a very unsatisfactory food to such appetites at that time. They went to bed, however, and lived in hope as long as the fast lasted.

Those who ate these little suppers, I am assured, never fasted.

The *chef-d'oeuvre* of a kitchen of those days, I am assured, was a strictly apostolic collation, which, however, was very like a good supper.

Science soon resolved this problem by the recognition of fish, soups, and pastry made with oil. The observing of fasting, gave rise to an unknown pleasure, that of the Easter celebration.

A close observation shows that the elements of our enjoyment are, difficult privation, desire and gratification. All of these are found in the breaking of abstinence. I have seen two of my grand uncles, very excellent men, too, almost faint with pleasure, when, on the day after Easter, they saw a ham, or a pate brought on the table. A degenerate race like the present, experiences no such sensation.

ORIGIN OF THE REMOVAL OF RESTRICTION IN FASTING

I witnessed the rise of this. It advanced by almost insensible degrees.

Young persons of a certain age, were not forced to fast, nor were pregnant women, or those who thought themselves so. When in that condition, a soup, a very great temptation to those who were well, was served to them.

Then people began to find out that fasting disagreed with them, and kept them awake. All the little accidents man is subject to were then attributed to it, so that people did not fast, because they thought themselves sick, or that they would be so. Collations thus gradually became rarer.

This was not all; some winters were so severe that people began to fear a scarcity of vegetables, and the ecclesiastical power officially relaxed its rigor.

The duty, however, was recognized and permission was always asked. The priests were refused it, but enjoined the necessity of extra alms giving.

The Revolution came, which occupied the minds of all, that none thought of priests, who were looked on as enemies to the state.

This cause does not exist, but a new one has intervened. The hour of our meals is totally changed; we do not eat so often, and a totally different household arrangement would be required for fasting. This is so true, that I think I may safely say, though I visit none but the best regulated houses, that, except at home, I have not seen a lenten table, or a collation ten times in twenty- five years.

We will not finish this chapter without observing the new direction popular taste has taken.

Thousands of men, who, forty years ago would have passed their evenings in *cabarets*, now pass them at the theatres.

Economy, certainly does not gain by this, but morality does. Manners are improved at the play, and at *cafés* one sees the journals. One certainly escapes the quarrels, diseases, and degradation, which infallibly result from the habit of frequenting *cabarets*.

MEDITATION XXV

EXHAUSTION

BY exhaustion, a state of weakness, languor or depression, caused by previous circumstances is understood, rendering the exercise of the vital functions more difficult. There are various kinds of exhaustion, caused by mental labor, bodily toil and the abuse of certain faculties.

One great remedy is to lay aside the acts which have produced this state, which, if not a disease, approximates closely to one.

TREATMENT

After these indispensable preliminaries, gastronomy is ready with its resources.

When a man is overcome by too long fatigue, it offers him a good soup, generous wine, flesh and sleep.

To a savant led into debility by a too great exercise of his mental faculties, it prescribes fresh air, a bath, fowl and vegetables.

The following observation will explain how I effected a cure of another kind of exhaustion.[36]

CURE BY THE PROFESSOR

J'allai un jour faire visite a un de mes meilleurs amis (M. Rubat); on me dit qu'il etait malade, et effectivement je le trouvai en robe de chambre aupres de son feu, et en attitude d'affaissement.

Sa physionomie m'effraya: il avait le visage pale, les yeux brillants et sa levre tombait de maniere a laisser voir les dents de la machoire inferieure, ce qui avait quelque chose de hideux.

---

[36] The translator thinks it best not to translate this anecdote, but merely to append the original.

Je m'enquis avec interet de la cause de ce changement subit; il hesita, je le pressai, et apres quelque resistance: "Mon ami, dit- il en rougissant, tu sais que ma femme est jalouse, et que cette manie m'a fait passer bien des mauvais moments. Depuis quelques jours, il lui en a pris une crise effroyable, et c'est en voulant lui prouver qu'elle n'a rien perdu de mon affection et qu'il ne se fait a son prejudice aucune derivation du tribut conjugal, que je me suis mis en cet etat.–Tu as donc oublie, lui dis-je, et que tu as quarante-cinq ans, et que la jalousie est un mal sans remede? Ne sais-tu pas furens quid femina possit?" Je tins encore quelques autres propos peu galants, car j'étais en colere.

"Voyons, au surplus, continuai-je: ton pouls est petit, dur, concentre; que vas-tu faire?–Le docteur, me dit-il, sort d'ici; il a pense que j'avais une fievre nerveuse, et a ordonne une saignee pour laquelle il doit incessamment m'envoyer le chirurgien.–Le chirurgien! m' ecriai-je, garde-t'en bien, ou tu es mort; chasse-le comme un meurtrier, et dis lui que je me suis empare de toi, corps et ame. Au surplus, ton medecin connait-il la cause occasionnelle de ton mal?–Helas! non, une mauvaise honte m'a empeché de lui fairs une confession entiere.–Eh bien, il faut le prier de passer cher toi. Je vais te faire une potion appropriee a ton etat; en attendant prends ceci." Je lui presentai un verre d'eau saturee de sucre, qu'il avala avec la confiance d'Alexandre et la foi du charbounier.

Alors je le quittai et courus chez moi pour y mixtionner, fonctionner et elaborer un magister reparateur qu'on trouvera dans les Variétés, avec les divers modes que j'adoptai pour me hater; car, en pareil cas, quelques heures de retard peuvent donner lieu a des accidents irreparables.

Je revins bientot arme de ma potion, et deja je trouvai du mieux; la couleur reparaissait aux joues, l'oeil etait detendu; mais la levre pendait toujours avec une effrayante difformite.

Le medecin ne tarda pas a reparaitre; je l'instruisis de ce que j'avais fait et le malade fit ses aveux. Son front doctoral prit d'abord un aspect severe; mais bientot nous regardant avec un air ou il y avait un peu d'ironie: "Vous ne devez pas etre etonne, dit-il a mon ami, que je n'aie pas devine une maladie qui ne convient ni a votre age ni a votre etat, et il y a de votre part trop de modestie a en cacher la cause, qui ne pouvait que vous faire honneur. J'ai encore a vous gronder de ce que vous m'avez expose a une erreur qui aurait pu vous etre funeste. Au surplus, mon confrere, ajouta-til en me faisant un salut que je lui rendis avec usure, vous a indique la bonne route; prenez son potage, quel que soit le nom qu'il y donne, et si la fievre vous quitte, comme je le crois, dejeunez demain avec une tasse de chocolat dans laquelle vous ferez delayer deux jaunes d'oeufs frais."

A ces mots il prit sa canne, son chapeau et nous quitta, nous laissant fort tentés de nous égayer a ses dépens.

Bientôt je fis prendre a mon malade une forte tasse de mon elixir de vie; il le but avec avidite, et voulait redoubler; mais j'exigeai un, ajournement de deux heures, et lui servis une seconde dose avant de me retirer.

Le lendemain il était sans fievre et presque bien portant; il dejeuna suivant l'ordonnance, continua la potion, et put vaquer des le surlendemain a ses occupations ordinaires; mais la levre rebelle ne se releva qu'apres le troisieme jour.

Peu de temps apres, l'affaire transpira, et toutes les dames en chuchotaient entre elles.

Quelques-unes admiraient mon ami, presque toutes le plaignaient, et le professeur gastronome fut glorifié.

MEDITATION XXVI

DEATH

Omnia mors poscit; lex est, non poena, perire.

God has subjected man to six great necessities: birth, action, eating, sleep, reproduction and death.

Death is the absolute interruption of the sensual relations, and the absolute annihilation of the vital powers, which abandons the body to the laws of decomposition.

These necessities are all accompanied and softened by a sensation of pleasure, and even death, when j natural, is not without charms. We mean when a man has passed through the different phases of growth, virility, old age, and decrepitude.

Had I not determined to make this chapter very short, I would invoke the assistance of the physicians, who have observed every shade of the transition of a living to an inert body. I would quote philosophers, kings, men of letters, men, who while on the verge of eternity, had pleasant thoughts they decked in the graces; I would recall the dying answer of Fontinelle, who being asked what he felt, said, "nothing but the pain of life;" I prefer, however, merely to express my opinion, founded on analogy as sustained by many instances, of which the following is the last:

I had a great aunt, aged eighty-three when she died. Though she had long been confined to her bed, she preserved all her faculties, and the approach of death was perceived by the feebleness of her voice and the failing of her appetite.

She had always exhibited great devotion to me, and I sat by her bed-side anxious to attend on her. This, however, did not prevent my observing her with most philosophic attention.

"Are you there, nephew?" said she in an almost inaudible voice. "Yes, aunt! I think you would be better if you would take a little old wine." "Give it to me, liquids always run down." I hastened to lift her up and gave her half a glass of my best and oldest wine. She revived for a moment and said, "I thank you. If you live as long as I have lived, you will find that death like sleep is a necessity."

These were her last words, and in half an hour she had sank to sleep forever.

Richerand has described with so much truth the gradations of the human body, and the last moments of the individual that my readers will be obliged to me for this passage.

"Thus the intellectual faculties are decomposed and pass away. Reason the attribute of which man pretends to be the exclusive possessor first deserts him. He then loses the power of combining his judgment, and soon after that of comparing, assembling, combining, and joining together many ideas. They say then that the invalid loses his mind, that he is delirious. All this usually rests on ideas familiar to the individual. The dominant passion is easily recognized. The miser talks most wildly about his treasures, and another person is besieged by religious terrors.

"After reasoning and judgment, the faculty of association becomes lost. This takes place in the cases known as *defaillances*, to which I have myself been liable. I was once talking with a friend and met with an insurmountable difficulty in combining two ideas from which I wished to make up an opinion. The syncopy was not, however, complete, for memory and sensation remained. I heard the persons around me say distinctly he is fainting, and sought to arouse me from this condition, which was not without pleasure.

"Memory then becomes extinct. The patient, who in his delirium, recognized his friends, now fails even to know those with whom he had been on terms of the greatest intimacy. He then loses sensation, but the senses go out in a successive and determinate order. Taste and smell give no evidence of their existence, the eyes become covered with a mistful veil and the ear ceases to execute its functions. For that reason, the ancients to be sure of the reality of death, used to utter loud cries in the ears of the dying. He neither tastes, sees, nor hears. He yet retains the sense of touch, moves in his bed, changes the position of the arms and body every moment, and has motions analogous to those of the foetus in the womb. Death affects him with no terror, for he has no ideas, and he ends as he begun life, unconsciously. "(*Richerand's Elements on Physiology,* vol. ii. p. 600.)

MEDITATION XXVII

PHILOSOPHICAL HISTORY OF THE KITCHEN

COOKERY is the most ancient of arts, for Adam must have been born hungry, and the cries of the infant are only soothed by the mother's breast.

Of all the arts it is the one which has rendered the greatest service in civil life. The necessities of the kitchen taught us the use of fire, by which man has subdued nature.

Looking carefully at things, three kinds of cuisine may be discovered.

The first has preserved its primitive name.

The second analyzes and looks after elements: it is called chemistry.

The third is the cookery of separation and is called pharmacy.

Though different objects, they are all united by the fact that they use fire, furnaces, etc., at the same time.

Thus a morsel of beef, which the cook converts into potage or *bouilli*, the chemist uses to ascertain into how many substances it may be resolved.

ORDER OF ALIMENTATION

Man is an omnivorous animal: he has incisors to divide fruits, molar teeth to crush grain, and canine teeth for flesh. Let it he remarked however, that as man approaches the savage state, the canine teeth are more easily distinguishable.

The probability was, that the human race for a long time, lived on fruit, for it is the most ancient food of the human race, and his means of attack until he had acquired the use of arms are very limited. The instinct of perfection attached to his nature, however, soon became developed, and the sentiment attached to his instinct was soon exhibited, and he made weapons for himself. To this he was impelled by a carniverous instinct, and he began to make prey of the animals that surrounded him.

This instinct of destruction yet exists: children always kill the animals that surround them, and if they were hungry would devour them.

It is not strange that man seeks to feed on flesh: He has too small a stomach, and fruit has not nourishment enough to renovate him. He could subsist on vegetables, but their preparation requires an art, only reached after the lapse of many centuries.

Man's first weapons were the branches of trees, and subsequently bows and arrows.

It is worthy of remark, that wherever we find man, in all climates and latitudes, he has been found with and arrows. None can see how this idea presented itself to individuals so differently placed: it must be hidden by the veil of centuries.

Raw flesh has but one inconvenience. Its viscousness attaches itself to the teeth. It is not, however, disagreeable. When seasoned with salt it is easily digested, and must be digestible.

A Croat captain, whom I invited to dinner in 1815, was amazed at my preparations. He said to me, "When in campaign, and we become hungry, we knock over the first animal we find, cut off a steak, powder it with salt, which we always have in the sabretasche, put it under the saddle, gallop over it for half a mile, and then dine like princes."

When the huntsmen of Dauphiny go out in Septemher to shoot, they take both pepper and salt with them. If they kill a very fat bird they pluck, season it, carry it some time in their caps and eat it. They say it is the best way to serve it up.

If our ancestors ate raw food we have not entirely gotten rid of the habit. The most delicate palates like Aries' sausages, etc., which have never been cooked, but which are not, on that account, the less appetising.

DISCOVERY OF FIRE

Subsequently to the Croat mode, fire was discovered. This was an accident, for fire is not spontaneous. Many savage nations have been found utterly ignorant of it.

BAKING

Fire having been discovered it was made use of to perfect food; at first it was made use of to dry it, and then to cook it.

Meat thus treated was found better than when raw. It had more firmness, was eaten with less difficulty, and the osmazome as it was condensed by carbonization gave it a pleasing perfume.

They began, however, to find out that flesh cooked on the coals became somewhat befouled, for certain portions of coal will adhere to it. This was remedied by passing spits through it, and placing it above burning coals at a suitable height.

Thus grillades were invented, and they have a flavor as rich as it is simple. All grilled meat is highly flavored, for it must be partially distilled.

Things in Homer's time had not advanced much further, and all will be pleased here to read the account of Achilles' reception of the three leading Greeks, one of whom was royal.

I dedicate this story to the ladies, for Achilles was the handsomest of all the Greeks, and his pride did not prevent his weeping when Briseis was taken from him, viz:[37]

The following is a translation by Pope:

"Patroclus, crown a larger bowl, Mix purer wine, and open every soul. Of all the warriors yonder host can send, Thy friend most honours these, and these thy friend."

He said: Patroclus o'er the blazing fire Heaps in a brazen vase three chines entire: The brazen vase Automedon sustains, 'Which flesh of porket, sheep, and goat contains: Achilles at the genial feast presides, The parts transfixes, and with skill divides. Meanwhile Patroclus sweats the fire to raise; The tent is brightened with the rising blaze:

Then, when the languid flames at length subside, He strews a bed of glowing embers wide, Above the coals the smoking fragments turns And sprinkles sacred salt from lifted urns; With bread the glittering canisters they load. Which round the board Menoetius' son bestow'd: Himself, opposed to Ulysses, full in sight, Each portion parts, and orders every rite. The first fat offerings, to the immortals due, Amid the greedy Patroclus threw; Then each, indulging in the social feast, His thirst and hunger soberly

---

[37] Verse in Greek omitted

repress'd. That done, to Phoenix Ajax gave the sign; Not unperceived; Ulysses crown'd with wine The foaming bowl, and instant thus began, His speech addressing to the godlike man: "Health to Achilles!"

Thus then a king, a son of a king, and three Grecian leaders dined very comfortably on bread, wine, and broiled meat.

We cannot but think that Achilles and Patroclus themselves prepared the entertainment, if only to do honor to the distinguished guests they received. Ordinarily the kitchen business was abandoned to slaves and women, as Homer tells us in Odyssey when he refers to the entertainment of the heralds.

The entrails of animals stuffed with blood were at that time looked on as very great delicacies.

At that time and long before, beyond doubt, poetry and music, were mingled with meals. Famous minstrels sang the wonders of nature, the loves of the gods, and warlike deeds of man. Theirs was a kind of priesthood and it is probable that the divine Homer himself was sprung from one of those men favored by heaven. He would not have been so eminent had not his poetical studies begun in his childhood.

Madame Dacier observes that Homer does not speak of boiled meat anywhere in his poems. The Jews had made much greater progress in consequence of their captivity in Egypt. They had kettles. Esau's mess of potage must have been made thus. For this he sold his birthright.

It is difficult to say how men learned the use of metals. Tubal Cain, it is said, was the inventor.

In the present state of knowledge, we use one metal to manufacture another. We overcome them with iron pincers; cut them with steel files, but I never met with any one who could tell me who made the first file or pair of pincers.

ORIENTAL ENTERTAINMENTS.–GRECIAN

Cookery made great advances. We are ignorant however of its utensils, whether of iron, pottery or of tin material.

The oldest books we know of make honorable mention of oriental festivals. It is not difficult to believe that monarchs who ruled such glorious realms abounded in all that was grateful. We only know that Cadmus who introduced writing into Greece, was cook of the king of Sidon.

The idea of surrounding the table with couches, originated from this voluptuous prince.

Cookery and its flavors were then highly esteemed by the Athenians, a people fond of all that was new. From what we read in their histories, there is no doubt but that their festivals were true feasts.

The wines of Greece, which even now we find excellent, have been estimated by scientific gourmands the most delicious that were.

The most beautiful women that ever came to adorn our entertainments were Greeks, or of Grecian origin.

The wisest men of old were anxious to display the luxury of such enjoyments. Plato, Atheneus, and many others, have preserved their names. The works of all of them, however, are lost, and if any remember them, it is only those who have heard of a long forgotten and lost book, the Gastronomy —the friend of one of the sons of Pericles.

Such was the cookery of Greece, which sent forth a few men who first established themselves in the Tiber, and then took possession of the world.

ROMAN FESTIVALS

Good cheer was unknown to the Romans as long as they thought to preserve their independence or to overcome their neighbors, who were poor as they were. Their generals therefore lived on vegetables. Historians have never failed to praise these times, when frugality was a matter of honor. When, however, their conquests had extended into Africa, Sicily and Hellas, when they had to live as people did where civilization was more advanced, they brought back to Rome the tastes which had attended them in foreign lands.

The Romans sent to Athens a deputation charged to bring back the laws of Solon. They also sent them thither to study *belles lettres* and philosophy. While their manners became polished they became aware of the attractions of festivals. And poets, philosophers, orators, etc., all came to Rome at once.

As time advanced, and as the series of events attracted to Rome almost all the riches of the world, the luxury of the table became incredible.

Every thing was eaten—the grasshopper and the ostrich, the squirrel and the wild boar—all imaginable vegetables were put in requisition.

Armies and travelers put all the world in requisition. The most distinguished Roman citizens took pleasure, not only in the cultivation of fruits once known, such as pears, apples, etc., but sought out things Lucullus never dreamed of. These importations which naturally had a great influence, prove at least that the impulse was general, that each one sought to contribute to the enjoyment of those around him.

Our drinks were not the object of less attention, nor of less attentive cares. The Romans were delighted with the wines of Italy, Greece, and Sicily. As they estimated their value from the year in which they were made, we may understand Cicero's much abused line,

Oh tortuna tam, natura, me consule Roman.

This was not all. In consequence of an instinct hitherto referred to, an effort was made to make them more highly perfumed, and flowers, aromatics, etc., were infused. Such things which the Romans called condita, must have had a very bad effect on the stomach.

Thus the Romans came to dream of alcohol, which was not discovered until long after they were born.

RESURRECTION OF LUCULLUS

The glorious days of old might arise again, and nothing but a Lucullus is needed, to bring this about. Let us fancy that any man, known to be rich, should wish to celebrate any great act, and give in this manner an occasion for a famous entertainment.

Let us suppose that he appeals to every one to adorn his entertainment, and orders every possible resource to be prepared.

Let him make every imaginable preparation and Lucullus would be as nothing compared with the civilized world as it is.

Both the Romans and the Athenians had beds to eat on. They achieved the purpose but indirectly.

At first they used beds only for the sacred festivals offered to the gods. The magistrates and principal men, adopted the custom, and ere long, it became general and was preserved until in the beginning of the fourth century.

These couches were at first, only boxes filled with straw, and covered with skins. Gradually, however, they became more luxurious, and were made of the most precious woods, inlaid with ivory, and sometimes with gems. Their cushions were soft and their covers magnificently embroidered.

People only laid down on the left elbow. Three usually slept together.

This the Romans called *lectisternium*. It is not a very bad name.

In a physical point of view incubation demands a certain exhibition of power to preserve equlibrium, and is not without a degree of pain; the elbow supporting an undue proportion of the weight of the body.

In a physiological point of view, something also is to be said. Imbuccation (swallowing) is effected in a less natural manner. The food is passed with more difficulty into the stomach.

The ingestion of liquids, or drinking, is yet more difficult. It required particular attention not to spill the wine from the large cups on the tables of the great. Thence came the proverb:

> "Between the cup and lip,
> There is often time a slip."

None could eat comfortably when reclining, especially when we remember that many of the guests had long beards, and that fingers, or at least only knives were used. Forks are an invention of modern times, for none were found at Herculaeneum.

Some violations of modesty must also have occurred at repasts which frequently exceeded the bounds of temperance, and where the two sexes have fallen asleep, and were mingled together. A poet says:

> "Nam pransus, jaceo, et satur supinus,
> Pertimdo tunicamque, palliumque."

When Christianity had acquired some power, its priests lifted up their voices against intemperance. They declaimed against the length of meals which violated all prudence by surrounding persons by every species of voluptuousness. Devoted by choice to an austere regimen, they placed gourmandise in the list of capital sins, and rigidly commented on the mingling of sexes and the use of beds, a habit which they said produced the luxury they deplored.

Their menacing voice was heard; couches disappeared, and the old habit of eating sitting, was restored. Fortunately this did not violate the demands of pleasure.

POETRY

Convivial poetry then underwent a new modification, and in the mouths of Horace and Tibullus assumed a languor the Greeks were ignorant of.

Dulce ridentem Lalagem amabo,
Dulce luquentem.
HOR.

Quaeris quot mihi batiationes
Tuae, Lesbia, sint satis superque.
CAT.

Pande, puella, pande capillulos
Mavos, lucentus ut aurum nitidum.
Pande, puella, collum candidum
Productum bene candidis humeris.
GALLUS.

IRRUPTION OF THE BARBARIANS

The five or six centuries we shall run over in a few pages, were glorious days for the cuisine; the irruption however of northern men overturned and destroyed everything.

When the strangers appeared, alimentary art made its appearance, as did the others that are its companions. The greater portion of the cooks were massacred in the palaces they served. The foreigners came and they were able to eat as much in an hour as civilized people did in a week.

Although that which is excessive is not durable—conquerors are always cruel. They united themselves with the victors, who received some tints of civilization, and began to know the pleasures of civilized life.

* * * * * * *

About the seventeenth century, the Dutch imported coffee into Europe. Solyman Agu, a Turk, whom our great, great grandfathers well remember, sold the first cups in 1760. An American sold it in 1670, and dealt it out from a marble bar, as we see now.

The use of coffee then dates from the eighteenth century. Distillation, introduced by the crusades, remained arcana, with few adepts. About the commencement of the reign of Louis XIV, alambics became more common, but not until the time of Louis XV., did the drink become really popular.

About the same time the use of tobacco was introduced. So that sugar, coffee and tobacco, the three most important articles of luxury in Europe, are scarcely two centuries old.

[The translator here omits a whole Meditation. It would now be scarcely pleasant.]

MEDITATION XXVIII

RESTAURATEURS

A restaurateur is one, the business of whom is to offer a dinner always ready, and with prices to suit those that consume them.

Of all those who frequent restaurants, few persons cannot understand that a restorateur is not necessarily a man of genius.

We shall follow out the affiliation of ideas which has led to the present state of affairs.

ESTABLISHMENT

About 1770, after the glorious days of Louis XIV., and the frolics and tranquility of the regency of Cardinal Fleury, foreigners had few means of good cheer.

They were forced to have recourse to innkeepers, the cookery of whom was generally very bad. A few hotels kept a *table d'hôte* which generally contained only what was very necessary, and which was always ready at an appointed hour.

The people we speak of only ordered whole joints, or dishes, and consequently such an order of things could not last.

At last a man of sense arose, who thought that an active cause must have its effect. That as the same want sent people every day to his house, consumers would come whenever they were satisfied that they would be served. They saw that if a wing was cut from a fowl for one person, some one would be sure to taste the thigh. The separation of one limb would not injure the flavor of the rest of the animal. More pay the least attention to the increase of prices, when one considers the prompt service of what was served.

This man thought of many things, which we may now easily devise. The one who did so was the first restaurateur and the inventor of a business which is a fortune to all who exercise it promptly and honorably.

[The translator here omits a whole chapter.]

From the examination of the bills of fare of different restaurants, any one who sets down at the table, has the choice of the following dishes:–

12 soups.

24 side dishes.

15 or 20 preparations of beef.

20 of mutton.

30 of fowl or game.

16 or 20 of veal.

12 of pastry.

24 of fish.

15 roasts.

50 side dishes.

50 desserts.

Besides the fortunate gastronomer has thirty kinds of wine to select from, passing over the whole scale from Burgundy to Tokay, and Constantia, and twenty various kinds of essences, without taking into consideration such mixed drinks as punch, negus, sillabubs and the like.

Of the various parts of a good dinner, many are indigenous, such as butcher's meat, fowl and fruits. Others for instance, the beef- stake, Welch rare-bit, punch, etc., were invented in England. Germany, Spain, Italy, Holland, all contribute, as does India, Persia, Arabia, and each pay their quota, in sour-krout, raisins, parmera, bolognas, curacao, rice, sago, soy, potatoes, etc. The consequence is, that a Parisian dinner is perfectly cosmopolitan.

[The translator here omits two Meditations, which refer exclusively to Paris is 1825. Few Frenchmen NOW would understand them, and none but a Frenchman could.]

PHYSIOLOGY OF TASTE

PART SECOND

TRANSITION

If I have been read with the attention I wished, all must have seen that I had a double purpose in view. The first was to establish the theoretical basis of Gastronomy, so as to place it among sciences where it should doubtless be. The second was to define gourmandise, and to separate this social character, as free from gluttony and intemperance, with which it is often confounded.

This *equivoque* has been introduced by intolerant moralists, who, deceived by too much zeal, saw excesses where there was only innocent enjoyment. The treasures of creation were not made to be trodden under the feet. It was afterwards propagated by grammarians who defined it as blind men do, and who swore in *verba magistri*.

It is time that such an error should cease, for now all the world understand each other. This is true, for there never was a person who would not confess to some tincture of gourmandise, and even would not boast of it, none however would not look on gluttony as an insult, just as they do on intemperance and voracity.

About these two cardinal points, it seems that what I have described should satisfy all those who do not refuse conviction. I might then lay down my pen and look on the task I have imposed on myself as finished. As however, I approached those subjects which belong to every thing, I remembered many things which it did not seem to me fit to write, such as anecdotes, bon mots, recipes, and other odd things.

Had they been put in the theoretical portion of the book they would have taken the connection; place them all together, they will not be disadvantageous because they contain some experimental truths and useful explanations.

I have also inserted personal biography, but when I read them over, I feel to a degree uneasy.

This anxiety originated in my last lectures and glossaries, which are in the hands of every body. I think, however, that I may be tranquil, having sheltered myself under the mantle of philosophy, I insist that my enemies have uneasy consciences and sleep badly.

VARIETIES

I

L'OMELETTE DU CURE

All know that twenty years ago, Madame R–– was the most beautiful woman in Paris. All know that she was very charitable and took an interest in the various enterprises, the object of which was the alleviation of misery, perhaps greater in the capital than elsewhere.

Having business with the cure of––, she went thither about five P. M., and was surprised to find him at dinner.

She believed that every body dined at six P. M., and was not aware that ecclesiastics dined earlier, from the fact that they were used to take light collations.

Madame R–– wished to retire, but the cure would not permit her to do so, either because the matter under discussion would not interrupt conversation, or that a pretty woman never disturbs any entertainment.

The table was very well arranged; old wine sparkled in a chrystal flagon, and the porcelain was faultless. The plates were kept hot by boiling water, and an old housekeeper was in attendance.

The meal was half way between luxury and abstinence. A soup of *ecrevisses* was removed and a salmon trout, an omelette, and a salad were placed on the table.

"My dinner tells you," said the priest "what you do not know, that to day is a fast day." My friend assented with a blush.

They began with the trout, the shoulders of which were soon eaten. The sauce was made by a competent person and the pastor's brow was irradiated with joy.

Then the omelette, which was round and done to a point, was attached.

As soon as the spoon touched it, the odor and perfume it contained cscaped, and my friend owns that it made her mouth water.

The curel had a sympathetic movement for he was used to watch my passions. In reply to a question he saw Madame R–– was about to ask, he said, "It is an *omelette au thon*. My cook understands them simply, and few people ever taste them without complimenting her." "I am not amazed," said his lady guest, "for I never ate anything so delightful."

Then came the salad. (I recommend it to those who have confidence in me. It refreshes without exciting. I think it makes people younger.)

Dinner did not interrupt conversation. They talked of the affair which had occasioned the visit, of the war, of business, of other things which made a bad dinner passably good.

The dessert came. It consisted of *septmoncel* cheese, of apples and preserves.

At last the housekeeper brought forward a little round table, such as once was called a *gueridon*, on which was a cup of strong mocha, the perfume of which filled the room.

Having sipped it, the cure said grace, and arose, adding "I never take spirits, though I offer them to my guests. I reserve them as a succor for extreme old age."

While all this was progressing, time had passed, and as it was six o'clock, Madame R–– was anxious to get into her carriage, for she had several friends to dine with her. She came late, and told her guests, of whom I was one, what she had seen.

The conversation passed from subject to subject, but I, as a philosopher, thought the secret of the preparation of such a dish must be valuable. I ordered my cook to obtain the recipe in its most minute details. I publish it the more willingly now, because I never saw it in any book.

OMELETTE AU THON

Take for six persons the roe of four cash[38] and steep them for a few minutes in salt water just below boiling point.

Put in also a fresh tunny about as large as an egg, to which you must add a charlotte minced.

Mix the tunny and the roes together, and put the whole in a kettle with a portion of good butter, and keep it on the fire until the butter has melted. This is the peculiarity of the omelette.

---

[38] The translator has followed this recipe with shad, pike, pickerel, etc., and can recommend it with a quiet conscience. Any fish is a substitute for tunny

Take then another piece of butter and mix it with parsely and sage. Put it in the dish intended to receive the omelette, cover it with lemon juice and put it on hot coals.

Then beat twelve eggs, (fresh as possible), pour in the fish and roe so that all may be perfectly mixed.

Then cook the omelette as usual, making it thin and firm. Serve it up hot.

This dish should be reserved for breakfasts, where all the guests are connoisseurs. It is caviare to the vulgar.

OBSERVATIONS

1. The roes and fish should be warmed, not boiled. They will thus mingle more easily with the eggs.

2. The plate should be deep.

3. It should be warm, for a cold porcelain plate would extract the caloric of the omelette and make it insipid.

II.

A NATIONAL VICTORY

When I lived in New York I used every once in a while to pass the evening in a kind of tavern kept by a man named Little, (*the old bank coffee house*) where one could always get turtle soup and all the dishes common in the United States.

I often went thither with the Vicomte de la Massue and M. Fehr, an old broker of Marsailles; all three of us were emigrants, and we used to drink ale and cider, and pass the evening very pleasantly together.

There I became acquainted with a Mr. Wilkinson, who was a native of Jamaica, and a person he was very intimate with, for he never left him. The latter, the name of whom I do not remember was one of the most extraordinary men I ever met. He had a square face, keen eyes, and appeared to look attentively at everything, though his features were motionless as those of a blind man. When he laughed it was with what the English call a horselaugh, and immediately resumed his habitual taciturnity. Mr. Wilkinson seemed about forty, and, in manner and appearance, seemed to be a gentleman.

The Englishman seemed to like our company, and more than once shared the frugal entertainment I offered my friends, when Mr. Wilkinson took me one evening aside and said he intended to ask us all to dine with him.

I accepted the invitation for three o'clock on the third day after.

The evening passed quietly enough, but when I was about to leave, a waiter came to me and said that the West Indian had ordered a magnificent dinner, thinking their invitation a challenge. The man with the horselaugh had undertaken to drink us Frenchmen drunk.

This intelligence would have induced me, if possible, to decline the banquet. It was, however, impossible, and following the advice of the Marshal de Saxe, we determined, as the wine was uncorked, to drink it.

I had some anxiety, but being satisfied that my constitution was young, healthy and sound, I could easily get the better of the West Indian, who probably was unused to liquors.

I however, went to see Messrs. Fehr and Massue, and in an occular allocution, told them of my plans. I advised them to drink as little as possible, and to avoid too many glasses, while I talked to our antagonists. Above all things, I advised them to keep up some appetite, telling them that food had the effect of moderating the fumes of wine.

Thus physically and morally armed, we went to the old bank coffee house, where we found our friends; dinner was soon ready. It consisted of a huge piece of beef, a roasted turkey, (plain) boiled vegetables, a salad and pastry.

Wine was put on the table. It was claret, very good, and cheaper than it then was in France.

Mr. Wilkinson did the honors perfectly, asking us to eat, and setting us an example, while his friend, who seemed busy with his plate, did nothing but laugh at the corners of his mouth.

My countrymen delighted me by their discretion.

After the claret came the port and Madeira. To the latter we paid great attention.

Then came the dessert composed of butter, cheese and hickory nuts. Then came the time for toasts, and we drank to our kings, to human liberty, and to Wilkinson's daughter Maria, who was, as he said, the prettiest woman in Jamaica.

Then came spirits, viz., rum, brandy, etc. Then came songs, and I saw things were getting warm. I was afraid of brandy and asked for punch. Little brought a bowl, which, doubtless, he had prepared before. It held enough for forty people, and was larger than any we have in France.

This gave me courage; I ate five or six well buttered rolls, and I felt my strength revive. I looked around the table and saw my compatriots apparently fresh enough, while the Jamaican began to grow red in the face, and seemed uneasy. His friend said nothing, but seemed so overcome that I saw the catastrophe would soon happen.

I cannot well express the amazement caused by this denouement, and from the burden of which I felt myself relieved. I rang the bell; Little came up; I said, "see these gentlemen well taken care of." We drank a glass to their health. At last the waiter came and bore off the defeated party feet foremost. Wilkinson's friend was motionless, and our host would insist on singing, "Rule Britannia."[39]

The New York papers told the story the next day, and added that the Englishman had died. This was not so, for Mr. Wilkinson had only a slight attack of the gout.

III

MYSTIFICATION OF THE PROFESSOR AND DEFEAT OF A GENERAL

Several years ago the newspapers told us of the discovery of a new perfume called the *emerocallis*, a bulbous plant, which has an odor not unlike the jasmin.

I am very curious, and was, therefore, induced in all probability to go to, the *Foubourg St. Germain*, where I could find the perfume.

I was suitably received, and a little flask, very well wrapped up, was handed me, which seemed to contain about two ounces. In exchange for it I left three francs.

An *etourdi* would at once have opened, smelled and tasted it. A professor, however, acts differently, and I thought modesty would become me. I took the flagon then and went quictly home, sat on my sofa and prepared to experience a new sensation.

---

[39] The translator is sorry to say, that at the time Savarin speaks of, "Rule Britannia" was not yet written.

I took the package from my pocket and untied the wrappings which surrounded it. They were three different descriptions of the *emerocallis*, and referred to its natural history, its flower, and its exquisite perfume, either in the shape of *pastilles*, in the kitchen, or in ices. I read each of the wrappings. 1. To indemnify myself as well as I could for the price I have spoken of above. 2. To prepare myself for an appreciation of the new and valuable extract I have spoken of.

I then opened, with reverence, the box I supposed full of pastilles. To my surprise, however, I found three other copies of the edition I had so carefully read. Inside I found about two dozen of the cubes I had gone so far for.

I tasted them, and must say that I found them very agreeable. I was sorry though, that they were so few in number, and the more I thought of the matter, the more I became mystified.

I then arose with the intention of carrying the box back to its manufacturer. Just then, however, I thought of my grey hairs, laughed at my vivacity, and sat down.

A particular circumstance also recurred to me. I had to deal with a druggist, and only four days ago I had a specimen of one of that calling.

I had one day to visit my friend *Bouvier des Eclats*.

I found him strolling in a most excited state, up and down the room, and crushing in his hands a piece of poetry, I thought a song.

He gave it to me and said, "Look at this, you know all about it."

I saw at once that it was an apothecary's bill. I was not consulted as a poet, but as a pharmaceutist.

I knew what the trade was, and was advising him to be quiet, when the door opened, and we saw a man of about fifty-five enter. He was of moderate stature and his whole appearance would have been stern, had there not been something sardonic about his lips.

He approached the fireplace, refused to sit down, and I heard the following dialogue I have faithfully recorded.

"Monsieur," said the general, "you sent me a regular apothecary's bill."

The man in black said that he was not an apothecary.

"What then are you?" said the general.

"Sir, I am a pharmaceutist."

"Well," said the general, "your boy–"

"Sir, I have no boy."

"Who then was the young man you sent thither?"

"My pupil–"

"I wish to say, sir, that your drugs–"

"Sir, I do not sell drugs–"

"What then do you sell?"

"Remedies."

The general at once became ashamed at having committed so many solicisms in a few moments, and paid the bill.

IV

THE SNARE

The chevalier de Langeac was rich, but his fortune was dispensed, as is the fortune of all rich men.

He funded the remnants, and aided by a little pension from the government, he contrived to lead a very pleasant life.

Though naturally very gallant, he had nothing to do with women.

As his other powers passed away, his *gourmandise* increased. He became a professor and received more invitations than he could accept.

Lyons is a pleasant city, for there one can get *vin de Bordeaux*, Hermitage and Burgundy. The game of the neighborhood is very good, and unexceptionable fish is taken from the lakes in the vicinity. Every body loves Bresse chickens.

Langeac was therefore welcome at all the best tables of the city, but took especial delight in that of a certain M. A.

In the winter of 1780, the chevalier received a letter, inviting him to sup ten days after date, (at that time I know there were suppers) and the chevalier quivered with emotion at the idea.

He, at the appointed time, made his appearance, and found ten guests. There was at that time no such A grand dinner was soon served, consisting of fish, flesh, and fowl.

All was very good, but the chevalier was not satisfied with the hopes he had entertained.

Another thing amazed him. His guests did not seem to eat. The chevalier was amazed to see that so many anti-convivial persons had been collected, and thinking that he had to do justice to all these fasting people set to work at once.

The second service was solid as the first. A huge turkey was dressed plain, flavored by salads and *macaroni au Parmesan*.

When he saw this, the chevalier felt his strength revive; all the other guests were overpowered, excited by the changes of wines, he triumphed over their impotence, and drank their health again and again. Every time he drank their health, he took a slice from the turkey.

Due attention was paid to the side-dishes, and the chevalier stuck to business longer than any one would have thought possible. He only revived when the *becfigues* appeared, and became fully aroused when truffles were put on the table.

THE TURBOT

Discord one day sought to affect an entrance into one of the most harmonious houses of Paris. A turbot was to be cooked.

The fish was on the next day to be served to a company of which I was one; it was fresh, fat, and glorious, but was so large that no dish in the house could hold it.

"Let us cut it in half," said the husband.

"Would you thus dishonor it?" said the wife.

"We must, my dear."

"Well, bring the knife, we will soon do it."

"Wait though, our cousin, who is a professor, will soon be here. He will relieve us from the dilemma."

The Gordian knot was about to be released, when I came in hungry, as a man always is at seven P. M.

When I came in I tried in vain to make the usual compliments. No one listened, and for that reason no one replied to me. The subject in discussion was at once submitted to me.

I made up my mind at once, went to the kitchen, found a kettle large enough to boil the whole fish, and did so. There was a procession composed of the master, mistress, servants, and company, but they all approved of what I did. With the fish we boiled bulbous root and other vegetables.[40]

When the fish was cooked we sat down at the table, our ideas being somewhat sharpened by the delay, and sought anxiously for the time, of which Homer speaks, when abundance expells hunger.[41]

VI

PHEASANTS

None but adepts know what a pheasant is. They only can appreciate it.

Everything has its apogee of excellence, some of which, like capers, asparagus, partridges, callow-birds, etc., are eatable only when they are young. Others are edible only when they obtain the perfection of their existence, such as melons and fruits, and the majority of the beasts which furnish us with animal food. Others are not good until decomposition begins, such as the snipe and pheasant.

When the pheasant is eaten only three days after its death, it has no peculiarity; it has not the flavor of a pullet, nor the perfume of a quail.

It is, however, a highly flavored dish, about half way between chicken and venison.

It is especially good when the pheasant begins to be decomposed– an aroma and exciting oil is then produced, like coffee, only produced by torrefaction.

This becomes evident by a slight smell and change of color. Persons possessed, however, of the instincts of gourmandise see it at once, just as a good cook knows whether he should take his bird from the spit or give it a turn or two more.

When the pheasant is in that condition it should he plucked, and not before.

The bird should then he stuffed, and in the following manner:

Take two snipe and draw them so as to put the birds on one plate, and the livers, etc., on another.

---

[40] From the above it is very clear that Brillat Savarin made what the late D. Webster called a "chowder."

[41] The translator here omits a very excellent recipe for a fish-chowder. Everybody knows it.

Take the flesh and mingle it with beef, lard and *herbes fines*, adding also salt and truffles enough to fill the stomach of the pheasant.

Cut a slice of bread larger, considerably, than the pheasant, and cover it with the liver, etc., and a few truffles. An anchovy and a little fresh butter will do no harm.

Put the pheasant on this preparation, and when it is boiled surround it with Florida oranges. Do not be uneasy about your dinner.

Drink burgundy after this dish, for long experience has taught me that it is the proper wine.

A pheasant served in this way is a fit dish for angels, if they visited the world as they did in Lot's day.

What I say, experience has already proved. A pheasant thus stuffed by Picard at La Grange[42] was brought on the table by the cook himself. It was looked on by the ladies as they would have looked at one of Mary Herbault's hats. It was scientifically tasted, and in the interim the ladies eyes shone like stars, and their lips became coral.

I did more than this; I gave a similar proof to the judges of the supreme court. They are aware that the toga is sometimes to be laid aside, and I was able to show to several that good CHEER was a fit companion and reward for the labors of the senate. After a few moments the oldest judge uttered the word excellent. All bowed, and the court adopted the decision. I had observed that the venerable old men seemed to take great delight in smelling the dish, and that their august brows were agitated by expressions of extreme serenity, something like a half smile hanging on their lips.

All this thing, however is naturally accounted for. The pheasant, itself, a very good bird, had imbibed the dressing and the flavor of the truffle and snipe. It thus becomes thrice better.

Thus of all the good things collected, every atom is appreciated and the consequence is, I think the pheasant fit for the table of a prince.

Parve, nec invideo, sine me liber, ibis in aulam.

---

[42] Does he refer to La Fayette's estate?

VII.

GASTRONOMICAL INDUSTRY OF THE EMIGRES

Toute Francaise, a ce que j'imagine,
Sait, bien ou mal faire, un peu de cuisine.
Belle Arsene, Act III

In a chapter written for the purpose, the advantages France derived from gourmandise in 1815, were fully explained. This was not less useful to *émigrés*; all those, who had any alimentary resources, received much benefit from it.

When I passed through Boston, I taught a cook, named Julien, who in 1794 was in his glory, how to serve eggs with cheese. Julien was a skilful lad, and had, he said, been employed by the Archbishop of Bourdeaux. This was to the Americans a new dish, and Julien in return, sent me a beautiful deer he had received from Canada, which those I invited to do honour to it, thought admirable.

Captain Collet also, in 1794 and 1795 earned much money by the manufacture of ices and sherbets.

Women always take care to enjoy any pleasures which are new to them. None can form an idea of their surprise. They could not understand how it could remain so cold, when the thermometer was at 26 [degrees] Réaumur.

When I was at Cologne, I found a Breton nobleman, who thought himself very fortunate, as the keeper of a public house; and I might multiply these examples indefinitely. I prefer however to tell of a Frenchman, who became very rich at London, from the skill he displayed in making salad.

He was a Limousin, and if I am not mistaken, was named Aubignac, or Albignac.

Poor as he was, he went, however, one day to dine at one of the first restaurants of London. He could always make a good dinner on a single good dish.

While he was discussing a piece of roast beef, five or six dandies sat at the next table, and one of them advanced and said, "Sir, they say your people excel in the art of making a salad. Will you be kind enough to oblige us?"

After some hesitation d'Albignac consented, and having set seriously to work, did his best.

While he was making his mixture, he replied frankly to questions about his condition, and my friend owned, not without a little blushing, that he received the aid of the English government, a circumstance which doubtless induced one of the young men to slip a ten pound bank bill into his hand.

He gave them his address, and not long after, was much surprised to receive a letter inviting him to come to dress a salad at one of the best houses in Grosvenor square.

D'Albignac began to see that he might draw considerable benefit from it, and did not hesitate to accept the offer. He took with him various preparations which he fancied would make his salad perfect as possible.

He took more pains in this second effort, and succeeded better than he had at first. On this occasion so large a sum was handed to him that he could not with justice to himself refuse to accept it.

The young men he met first, had exaggerated the salad he had prepared for them, and the second entertainment was yet louder in its praise. He became famous as "the fashionable salad-maker," and those who knew anything of satirical poetry remembered:

> Desir do nonne est un feu pui devore,
> Desir d'Anglaise est cent fois piri encore.

D'Albignac, like a man of sense, took advantage of the excitement, and soon obtained a carriage, that he might travel more rapidly from one part of the town to the other. He had in a mahogany case all the ingredients he required.

Subsequently he had similar cases prepared and filled, which he used to sell by the hundred.

Ultimately he made a fortune of 80,000 francs, which he took to France when times became more peaceful.

When he had returned to France, he did not hurry to Paris, but with laudable precaution, placed 60,000 francs in the funds, and with the rest purchased a little estate, on which, for aught I know, he now lives happily. His funded money paid him fifty per cent.

These facts were imparted to me by a friend, who had known D'Albignac in London, and who had met him after his return.

VIII.

RECOLLECTIONS OF THE EMIGRATION.

THE WEAVER

In 1794, M. de Rostaing, my cousin and friend, now military intendant at Lyons, a man of great talent and ability, and myself were in Switzerland.

We went to Mondon, where I had many relations, and was kindly received by the family of Troillet. I will never forget their hospitality.

I was there shown a young French officer who was a weaver, and who became one thus:–

This young man, a member of a very good family, was passing through Mondon, to join Condés army, and chanced to meet an old man with one of the animated heads usually attributed by painters to the companions of the famous Tell.

At their dessert, the officer did not conceal his situation, and received much sympathy from his new friend. The latter complained that at such an age, he had now to renounce all that was pleasant, and that every man should, as Jean Jacques, says, have some trade to support themselves in adversity.

The conversation paused there; and a short time after, he joined the army of Condé. From what he saw there, however, he saw he never could expect to enter France in that way.

Then he remembered the words of the weaver; and finally making up his mind, left the army, returned to Mondon, and begged the weaver to receive him as an apprentice.

On the next day the officer set to work, dining and sleeping with the weaver, and was so assiduous, that after six months, his master told him, he had nothing to teach him, thought himself repaid for the care he had bestowed, and that all he earned henceforth was his own profit.

When I was at Mondon, the new artisan had earned money enough to purchase a shop and a bed. He worked with great assiduity, and such interest was taken in him, that some of the first houses of the city enquired after him every day.

On Sunday, he wore his uniform, and resumed his social rights. As he was very well read, all took pleasure in his company, and he did not seem discontented with his fate.

THE STARVING

To this picture of the advantage of industry, I am about to add an altogether different one.

I met at Lausanne, an émigré from Lyons, who to avoid work used to eat but twice a week. He would have died beyond a doubt, if a merchant in the city had not promised to pay for his dinner every Sunday, and Wednesday of the week.

The émigré came always at the appointed time, and always took away a large piece of bread.

He had been living in this manner some three months, when I met him; he had not been sick, but he was so pale that it was sad to see him.

I was amazed that he would suffer such pain rather than work. I asked him once to dine with me, but did not repeat the invitation because I believe in obeying that divine precept, "By the sweat of thy brow shalt thou earn thy bread."

SOJOURN IN AMERICA

From Switzerland I went to America.

* * * * * *

ASPARAGUS

Passing one day in February, by the Palais Royal, I paused before the shop of Mme Chevet, the largest dealer in *comestibles* in Paris, who always wished me well. Seeing a large box of asparagus, the smallest of which was large as my finger, I asked the price. "Forty francs," said she. "They are very fine, but only a king or prince could eat at such a rate." "You are wrong sir," said she, "such things never go to palaces, but I will sell the asparagus.

"There are now in this city at least three hundred rich men, capitalists and financiers, retained at home by gout, colds, and doctors. They are always busy to ascertain what will revive them and send their valets out on voyages of discovery. Some one of them will remark this asparagus, and it will be bought. It may be, some pretty woman will pass with her lover, and say, 'what fine asparagus. How well my servant dresses it.' The lover then does not hesitate, and I will tell you a secret, that dear things are sold more easily than cheap ones."

As she spoke two fat Englishmen passed us. They seemed struck at once. One seized hold of the asparagus and without asking the price paid for it, and as he walked away whistled "God save the King."

"Monsieur," said Madame Chevet, "a thousand things like this happen every day."

FONDUE

Fondue is a soup dish, and consists only in frying eggs in cheese in proportions revealed by experience. I will give the recipe. It is a pleasant dish, quickly made and easily prepared for unexpected guests. I refer to it here only for my peculiar pleasure, and because it preserves the memory of things which the old men of Belley recollect.

Towards the end of the 17th century M. Madot became bishop of Belley, and took possession of the diocese.

Those to whom his reception had been confided had provided an entertainment worthy of the occasion, and made use of all the preparations then known in the kitchen, to welcome my lord.

There was an immense fondue, to which the prelate paid great attention; to the surprise of all he ate it with a spoon, instead of a fork, as people had been used to do.

All the guests looked at each other with a perceptible smile on every face. A bishop from Paris, however, must know how to eat. On the next day there was a great deal of gossip, and people that met at the corners, said "Well did you see how our bishop ate his fondue? I heard from a person who was present that he used a spoon!"

The bishop had some followers, innovators who preferred the spoon, but the majority preferred the fork, and an old granduncle of mine used to laugh as if he would die, as he told how M. de Madot ate fondue with a spoon.

RECIPE FOR FONDUE, COPIED FROM THE PAPERS OF M. TROLLET, BAILLI OF MONDON IN BERNE

Calculate the number of eggs in proportion to the guests.

Take one-third of the weight of Gruyere and one-sixth of the weight of butter.

Beat the eggs and mingle them with the butter and cheese in a *casserole*.

Put the kettle on a hot fire and stir it until the mixture is perfect. Put in more or less salt in proportion as the cheese is old or new. Serve it hot, with good wine, of which one should drink much. The feast will see sights.

DISAPPOINTMENT

All one day was quiet at the *Ecu de France*, between Bourg and Bresse, when the sound of wheels was heard, and a superb English berline drove up, on the box of which were two pretty Abigails, wrapped in blue and red cloths.

At the sight, which announced a nobleman on his travels, Chicot, that was his name, hurried to the door of the equipage. The wife stood at the door, the girls near by, while the boys from the stable hurried forward satisfied that they would receive a handsome gratuity.

The women were unpacked and there came from the berline, 1st, a fat Englishman, 2d, two thin, pale, red-haired girls, and 3d, a lady, apparently in the first stage of consumption.

The last spoke:

"Landlord," said she, "take care of the horses, give us a room and the women refreshments. All must cost only six francs; act accordingly."

Chicot put on his bonnet, madame went into the house, and the girls to their garrets.

The horses were, however, put into the stable, the Englishman read the papers, and the women had a pitcher of pure water. The ladies went up stairs. The six francs were received as a poor compensation for the trouble caused.

WONDERFUL EFFECTS OF A CLASSICAL DINNER

"Alas! how much I am to be pitied," said the elegiac voice of a gastronomer of the royal court of the Seine. "Hoping to be soon able to return home, I left my cook there; business detains me at Paris, and I have to depend on an old women the preparations of whom make me sick. Anything satisfies my wife and children, but I am made a martyr of the spit and pot."

Luckily a friend heard the complaint, who said, "You will not, my friend, be a martyr. Deign to accept a classical dinner to-morrow, and after a game of *piquet* we will bury all in the abyss of the past."

The invitation was accepted, the mystery was solved, and since the 23d June, 1825, the professor has been delighted at having one of his best friends in royal court.

EFFECT AND DANGER OF STRONG DRINKS

The artificial thirst we previously alluded to, is that which for the moment appeals to strong drinks as a momentary relief. It gradually becomes so habitual that those who grow used to it cannot do without it even through the night, and have to leave their bed to appease it.

This thirst then becomes a real disease, and when he has reached that point, it may safely be said that he has not two years to live.

I travelled in Holland with a rich Dantzick merchant, who had for fifty years kept the principal house for the sale of brandy.

"Monsieur," said he "none in France are aware of the importance of the trade in brandy, which for nearly a century my father and myself have carried on. I have watched with attention the workmen who yield to it as too many Germans do, and they generally die in the same manner."

"At first they take simply a glass in the morning, and for many years this suffices. It is a common habit with all workmen, and any one who did not indulge in it would be ridiculed by his companions. Then they double the dose, that is to say, take a glass at morning and night. Thus things continue about three years, when they begin to drink three times a day, and will only taste spirits in which highly scented herbs have been infused. Having reached that point, one may be sure they have not more than six months to live, for they go to the hospital and are seen no more."

CHEVALIERS AND ABBÉS

I have already referred to these categories of gourmandise destroyed by time.

As they disappeared thirty years since, few of the present generation ever saw them.

About the end of the century they will probably reappear, but as such a phenomenon demand the coincidence of many future contingencies, I think few who live will ever witness this palingenesia.

As a painter of manners I must give the last touch to my portrait, and will borrow the following passage from an author, who, I know, will refuse me nothing.

"The title of Chevalier was only correctly granted to persons who had been decorated, or to the younger sons of noble houses. Many of the Chevaliers of other families would take the title for themselves, and if they had education and good manners, none doubted the accolade.

"They were generally young, wore the sword vertically and kept a stiff upper lip. They gamed and fought and were a portion of the train of any fashionable beauty."

At the commencement of the revolution many of the Chevaliers joined the army of the émigrés, enlisted or dispersed. The few who survive can yet be recognized by their military air; almost all of them, however, have the gout.

When any noble family had many children, one was dedicated to the church; at first some benefice, barely sufficient to pay for the expenses of education, was obtained, and ultimately he became Prince, Abbé, or Bishop, as circumstances dictated.

This was the real Abbé; but many young men who disliked the perils of the Chevalier, called themselves Abbes when they came to Paris.

Nothing was so convenient, for, with a slight change of dress, they could appear as priests and the equals of anybody. There was a great advantage in this for every house had its Abbé.

They were generally small, round, well dressed and agreeable. They were gourmands, active and pleasant. The few that remain have become very devout and very fat.

None could be more comfortable than a rich prior or abbot. They had no superiors and nothing to do. If there be a long peace, the priors will turn up again, but unless there be a great change in the ecclesiastical organization, the Abbés are lost forever.

MISCELLANY.–WINE

"Monsieur," said an old marquise to me one day, "which do you like best, Burgundy or Bordeaux?" "Madame," said I, "I have such a passion for examining into the matter, that I always postpone the decision a week."

STRAWBERRIES

The Count de la Place recommends that strawberries should always be dressed with orange juice.

JUDGMENT

"He is not a man of mind," said the Count de M–– "Why?" "Ah! he does not eat pudding a la Richelieu, nor cutlets a *la Soubise*."

RAISINS

"Take a raisin–"
"No I thank you; I do not like wine in pills."

A DAY WITH THE BERNARDINES

It was about one A. M., on a fine summer night, and I set out after having been serenaded by many who took an interest in us. This was about 1782.

I then was the chief of a troop of amateur musicians All of whom were young and healthy.

"Monsieur," said the abbé of Saint Sulpice to me one day, and he drew me into a window reccss, "you would enjoy yourself very much if you come some day to play for us at Saint Bernard's. The Saints would be delighted."

I accepted the offer at once, for it seemed to promise us an agreeable evening. I nodded assent, and all were amazed.

Annuit, et totum nutu tremefecit olympum.

Every precaution had previously been taken, for we had yet to go four leagues, a distance sufficient to terrify the persons who had ascended Mont Martre.

The monastery was in a valley, enclosed on the west side by a mountain, and on the east by a hill that was not so high.

The eastern peak was crowned by a forest of immense pines. The valley was one vast prairie, and the beech grows much like the arrangements of an English garden.

We came about evenfall, and were received by the cellarer who had a nose very rich-like an obelisk.

"Gentlemen," said he, "our abbé will be glad when he hears you have come. He is yet in bed; but come with me, and you will see whether we have expected you or not."

We followed him, and besought him to take us to the refectory.

Amid the display of the table arose a pâté like a cathedral; on one side was a quarter of cold veal, artichokes, etc., were also on the eastern range.

There were various kinds of fruits, napkins, knives and plate; at the foot of the table were many attentive servants.

At one corner of the refectory was seen more than an hundred bottles, kept cool by a natural fountain. We could snuff the aroma of mocha, though in those venerable days none ever drank mocha so early in the morning.

The reverend cellarer for a time laughed at our emotion, and then spoke to us as follows:

"Gentlemen," said he, "I would be pleased to keep you company, but as yet I have not kept my mass. I ought to ask you to drink, but the mountain air dispenses the necessity. Receive, then, what we offer you. I must to matins."

He went to matins.

We did our best to eat up the abbe's dinner, but could not. People from Sirius might, but it was too much for us.

After dinner we dispersed. I crept into a good bed until mass; like the heroes of Rocroy, who slept until the battle began.

I was aroused by a great fat friar, who had nearly pulled my arm out of its socket, and went to the church where I found all at their posts.

We played a symphony at the offertory and sung a motet at the elevation, concluding with four wind instruments.

We contrived, in spite of the jests usually expended on amateurs, to get out of the difficulty very well.

We received with great benignity the praises heaped on us, and having received the abbot's thanks went to the table.

The dinner was such as people used to eat in the fifteenth century. There were few superfluities, but the choice of dishes was admirable. We had plain, honest, substantial stews, good meats, and dishes of vegetables, which made one regret they were not more general.

The dessert was the more remarkable, as it was composed of fruits not produced at that altitude. The gardens of Machuras, of Morflent and other places had contributed.

There was no want of *liqueurs*, but coffee needs a particular reference.

It was clear, perfumed and strong, but was not served in what are called *tasses* on the Seine, but in huge bowls, into which the monks dipped their lips and smacked them with delight.

After dinner we went to vespers, and between the psalms executed antiphones I prepared for the purpose. That style of music was then fashionable. I cannot say if mine was good or bad.

Our DAY being over, my orchestra was enabled to look and walk around. On my return the abbé said, "I am about to leave you, and will suffer you to finish the night. I do not think my presence at all importunate to the fathers; but I wish them to do as they please."

When the abbot had left, the monks drew more closely together, and a thousand jokes were told, not the less funny because the world knows nothing of them.

About nine a glorious supper was served, long in advance of the dinner.

They laughed, sang, told stories, and one of the fathers recited some very good verses he had himself composed.

At last a monk arose, and said, "Father Cellarer, what have you to say?"

"True," said the father, "I am not cellarer for nothing."

He left, and soon returned with three servitors, the first of whom brought some glorious fresh buttered toast. The others had a table on which was a sweetened preparation of brandy and water—vulgo, punch.

The new comers were received with acclamation; the company ate the toasts, drank the toddy, and when the abbey clock struck twelve, all went to their cells to enjoy a repose they had richly earned.

PROSPERITY EN ROUTE

One day I rode a horse I called *la Joie* through the It was at the worst era of the revolution, and I went to see Mr. Prot to obtain a passport which, probably, might save me from prison or the scaffold.

At about 11 P. M., I reached a little burg or village called Mont St. Vaudrey, and having first attended to my horse, was struck by a spectacle no traveler ever saw without delight.

Before a fire was a spit covered with cock quails and the rails that are always so fat. All the juice from the quails fell on an immense *rôtie* so built up that the huntsman's hand was apparent. Then came one of those leverets, the perfume of which Parisians have no faith in though they fill the room.

"Ah ha!" said I; "Providence has not entirely deserted me. Let us scent this perfume and die afterwards."

Speaking to the landlord who, while I was making my examinations, walked up and down the room, I said, "*Mon cher*, what can you give us for dinner?"

"Nothing very good, Monsieur. You can have potatoes. The beans are awful. I never had a worse dinner."

The landlord seemed to suspect the cause of my disappointment. I said, however, "for whom is all this game kept?"

"Alas, Monsieur," said he, "it is not mine but belongs to some lawyers and judges who have been here several days on a business which concerns a very rich old lady. They finished yesterday, and wish to celebrate the event by a revolt."

"Monsieur," said I, "be pleased to say that a gentleman asks the favor of being permitted to dine with them, that he will pay his portion of the expense, and also be much obliged to them."

He left me and did not return, but after a few minutes a little fat man entered, who hovered around the kitchen, lifted up the covers and disappeared.

"Ah, ha!" said I. The tiler has come to look at me. I began to hope, for I knew my appearance was not repulsive. My heart beat quickly as a candidate's does after the ballot-box is opened, and before he knows the result, when the landlord told me the gentlemen only waited for me to sit down.

I went at once, and was received in the most flattering manner.

The dinner was glorious, I will not describe it, but only refer to an admirable fricassée of chicken not often seen in such perfection in the country. It had so many truffles that it would have revived an old Titan.

We sang, danced, etc., and passed the evening pleasantly.[43]

H. ... DE P ...

I believe I am the first person who ever conceived the idea of a gastronomical academy. I am afraid, however, I was a little in advance of the day, as people may judge by what took place fifteen years afterwards.

The President, H. de P., the ideas of whom braved every age and era, speaking to three of the most enlightened men of his age, (Laplace, Chaptal, and Berthollet,) said "I look in the history of the discovery of a new dish, which prolongs our pleasures, as far more important than the discovery of a new star."

I shall never think science sufficiently honored until I see a cook in the first class of the institute.

The good old President was always delighted when he thought of his labor. He always wished to furnish me an epigraph, not like that which made Montesquieu a member of the academy. I therefore, wrote several verses about it, but to be copied.

Dans ses doctes travaux il fut infatigable;
Il eut de grands emplois, qu'il remplit dignement:
Et quoiqu'il filt profond, erudit et savant,
Il ne se crut jamais dispense d'etre aimable.

---

[43] The translator here omits half a dozen songs, which are essentially French, and which no one can do justice to in another tongue.

CONCLUSION

My work is now done, yet I am not a bit out of breath.

I could give my readers countless stories, but all is now over, and as my book is for all time, those who will read it now will know nothing of those for whom I write.

Let the Professor here end his work.

Fin

CPSIA information can be obtained at www.ICGtesting.com
Printed in the USA
LVOW01s0709180315

430961LV00010B/52/P